The Soul:

An Owner's Manual

The Soul:
An Owner's Manual

*Discovering the Life
of Fullness*

GEORGE JAIDAR

WITH A FOREWORD BY JOSEPH CHILTON PEARCE

PARAGON HOUSE
New York

First Edition, 1995

Published in the United States by

Paragon House
370 Lexington Avenue
New York, NY 10017

Library of Congress Cataloging-in-Publication Data

Jaidar, George, 1930–
The soul : an owner's manual : Discovering the Life of
Fullness / George Jaidar.—1st ed.
p.   cm.
Includes bibliographical references and index.
ISBN 1-55778-710-7
1. Spiritual life.   2. Mysticism.   I. Title.
BL624.J35   1994
291.4'4—dc20   94-31789
                                                         CIP

Manufactured in the United States of America

To Nazha Mansour Jaidar,
my beloved Tyta,
whose heart, body, and mind prepared me for this
and
To Malchia Sanford Olshan,
my beloved noodge,
who in heart, body, and mind strives to embody this

Contents

Foreword

༄ ༅

JOSEPH CHILTON PEARCE

*F*or generations we have needed a new framework and lexicon for talking about the human spirit, and here it is. Everything that I (and others of similar bent) have written has only groped, at best, toward what is spelled out here. With the power and assurance of personal knowing, rather than conjecture, and with an admirable simplicity and clarity of style, George Jaidar shares with us a revelation he experienced a quarter of a century ago. Further, he has lived, or "realized," that revelation ever since—as important an accomplishment, together with this resulting document, as any that has been achieved in our time.

Jaidar is a former academic, but a generalist with a wide-ranging curiosity and a deep sense of wonder that precluded his compromising with today's mandatory narrowing specialization. He easily blends psychology, cultural anthropology, philosophy, science, and conventional religious terminology, as needed, to help bridge the author-reader gap. Yet he needs and makes no references to "higher authority," "science says," or the usual crutches. And we should guard against our usual tendency to put new wine like this (and it *is* new) into the old wineskins of our standard conceptions.

The structure of the book leads us quite clearly and compellingly from our common cultural plight, a *Life of Survival*, as he calls it, into that most uncommon domain of the spirit, a *Life of Fullness*. Early on, Jaidar tackles our enculturation—that mindset for survival we are locked into from conception. He specifies three levels of this survival conditioning, each of which shapes a level of our awareness or consciousness. These are: first, *subsistence survival*, ancient and necessary; second, *successful survival*, our clever survival enhancements by which we try to predict and control everything; and third, the *harmonizing/aesthetic*, our attempts to bring accord to the inevitable discord that successful surviving breeds and/or create beauty amidst the tragedy a survival mentality brings on itself.

Discontinuous with these three levels of survival, and indeed with everything known, is a fourth level, the *Life of Fullness*. Jaidar shows why and how our usual attempted spiritual strivings unwittingly serve our survival conditioning, or "lower self-order of functioning," and thus miss the mark of the Life of Fullness. No one has ever made so keen and perceptive an analysis of the human condition.

Jaidar reveals how the very fabric of our history and mind-set—accounting for every facet of our lives, including our religions and philosophies—is woven by this survival mode, which also serves to limit us critically. Intended as only a "First Journey," or preparation, a Life of Survival is, sadly, the only journey to which the mass of humanity is directed or encouraged by their enculturation.

Fear and hope are the twin foundations of that First Journey, and Jaidar's analysis of these two interdependent conditionings is brilliant and original, as is his distinction between depression and despair. His concept of "embracing despair" as the way out, although initially disturbing, is one of the most powerful and liberating insights I have come across.

A "higher self-order of functioning" is within us, but requires a completely innovative approach, a "Second Journey." We are drawn toward this evolving maturation by a "Yearning," which is our very lifeline (or Umbilicum), but which is generally diverted to desires sparked by those fear/hope twins of our First Journey.

Jaidar's exploration of soul as an emergent process of our human nature is revolutionary and enlightening, a key to the practice he outlines for aligning one's self with that process. Eminently pragmatic, available, and rewarding, this practice rests on four simple questions and answers that graphically give the foundation for this Second Journey. In this I find strong ties with such masters as Meister Eckhart (the journey into the unknown) and Jean Pierre de Caussade (on the subtle "letting" or allowing by which the highest process gradually becomes one's own way).

This book has many strengths: its contemporary language; its inventive mind-set and conceptual nature; its emancipation from the shackles of religion (the "tie that binds too tightly"); and its power to open us to pure process, the unknown of creation itself. The practice Jaidar commends provides access, not to the closed archetype of a system or tradition, but to the openness of the absolutely unknown, creation as itself, a journey that forms anew for each one taking it. (This may be a decisive difference between Eastern systems, with their clear directives and steps, and the far more ambiguous, difficult-to-describe ways of the great Christian and Sufic contemplatives who are Jaidar's predecessors.)

Jaidar long insisted on anonymity, refused anything suggestive of a "following," and eschewed writing about matters of the spirit (which require action, not mere verbalization, in his view). But now, for reasons of his own, he has written (by hand) this astonishing document, thus going public, to our general good fortune. The extent to which you discover this fortune for yourself will depend on whether or not you act on what you read. And for that reader who does "get it" and acts on it, I can only rejoice.

Acknowledgments

While many individuals over the last twenty-five years have urged me to write such a book, I resisted successfully—until recently. With an inimitable, gentle persistence, Malchia Sanford Olshan, my loving companion of the last twenty-four years and extraordinary practitioner of what is written here, finally broke my resistance and persuaded me of the need for my spoken teachings to be in written form.

A gentle prod was lovingly provided regularly by my very good friend of the past thirty-seven years, Professor Webster Cotton, who continues to practice "educare" in, of all places, a university. Also, encouragement came from Malchia's son (and like a son to me), Joseph Olshan, a gifted writer, teacher, and well-published novelist, whose reading of the manuscript and whose suggestions were much appreciated.

My thanks go to Valerie Riddle and Barbara Uniker for their reading of the manuscript and valuable editing suggestions. I appreciated Todd Saunders, my nephew (also like a son to me), for his skillful help in selecting, and in orienting me to, my new computer and to word processing, which proved to be a boon for editing and rewriting (I now even use it for most of my writing.) My thanks go also to Laszlo Farkas and Elizabeth Farkas for their timely help in entering my handwritten manuscript to the computer. To John S. Niendorff, I am thankful for editing an early part of the manuscript so helpfully that I was able to write the rest of the book with more of an editor's mind.

To Joseph Chilton Pearce, for his gracious words and very caring deeds, I am deeply appreciative. And for an incisive final editing, as well as many excellent suggestions and other loving help in getting this book ready for publishing, I am so very grateful to Barbara Neighbors Deal.

Finally, I want to express my appreciation to Michael Giampaoli, my publisher at Paragon House, for his vote of confidence and courage in deciding to publish this work by a first-time author, as well as to Marybeth Tregarthen, their production manager, for navigating the complicated journey through final editing, design, and production so skillfully; to both of them for making it all such a pain-free adventure for this newcomer to publishing.

For those of you who perceive any originality in this work, I wish to acknowledge, with the utmost humility, my deepest gratitude to the true and ultimate Source for granting me this continually unfolding, timeless, most adventuresome revelation beginning, in my awareness, in what we designate as the year 1970.

Preface

⟨⟨❦⟩⟩

This book was not written for a mass audience, but rather
for a vanguard that will serve as a "saving remnant" of our
species. These people quite uneasily know who they are. They
are successful in their society, but not just in the usual sense.
They have mastered the skills requisite for successful survival,
irrespective of the occupational or career path they have taken,
so they know they can land on their feet regardless of the circumstances they encounter. However, they have gone a step further.
Not only do they consider themselves successful, but they have
also discovered and become well aware of the limits and illusoriness of this success. Their success did not lead to the promised
and anticipated fulfillment. Even when they paused to reflect on
this but then redoubled their efforts on the assumption that the
shortcoming in their success was purely quantitative, the hoped-
for fulfillment still remained elusive.

Returning to the embrace of their familiar belief system, religion, or a variant thereof, as well as joining groups and seminars,

seeking and following gurus, dropping out or retreating, or getting involved in psychological or spiritual self-help courses and books—although promising and even temporarily satisfying—also failed to fulfill them. Many might have settled for these limited measures on the assumption that they were just expecting too much out of this life, a viewpoint amply reinforced by all too many individuals and institutions of our society.

These few, this vanguard or saving remnant, will not settle for the meager existence that passes for a life for so many. Instead, they will trust their own impetus to fulfillment: *the still, small voice within*. Further, they will not abandon, in an emotional thrall or a leap of faith, their reflective intellect, a crowning achievement of *Homo sapiens*. But unlike so many intellectuals, they are willing to acknowledge the limits of earthbound human intellect and logic in a generative Cosmos that requires a willingness to go *beyond* the human mind as currently constituted while also subsuming it. Thus, they can become aware of, and will need to participate in, an evolving, emergent human consciousness. And they will refuse to be left behind for the reward of a few more socioeconomic trinkets or even for some possible transitory psychological highs of their present consciousness.

Our human condition, though rife with despair, is pointing us beyond despair to possibilities we need to explore, to potentials that have already been revealed to humanity through various sentinels of our evolutionary flow. Such explorations will require the greatest of openness and courage—the spiritual equivalent of climbing Mount Everest—but for which individuals choosing this ascent will find themselves well-endowed. Humankind, although beyond religion and ready to go on in its spiritual development, hangs on to what must be described as a well-worn habit needing to be transcended in the Post-religious Era. Thus, the original subtitle of this book was *The Theory and Practice of Emergent Human Nature and Consciousness in the Post-religious Era*. (That was thought to be overly long and to sound a bit too academic.) However, as you will see, this is a most accurate description of this venture.

Although human consciousness seems to have evolved gradually and with continuity, it is at least equally plausible that it *also* evolved by leaps or discontinuities that we call mutations. We shall soon see that such a mutation has recently (in human evolutionary terms) become available as a conscious life choice for those who have the strength and confidence to claim and enter into it. This book was written for those intrepid explorers who are ready and willing to embark on such an adventure of consciousness and, as we shall see, concomitant action as well.

I

THE CHALLENGE

*T*he world in which we find ourselves—that upon which we immodestly confer the term *reality*—is not our natural milieu. This is a man-made contrivance earnestly designed to further our survival. It is based upon values and purposes conservatively grounded in what has worked in the past and been judged to have survival value for both society and the individual. We have used a variety of terms to refer to this reality, such as *worldview, framework, metaphysics*, and the German *Weltanschauung*, as well as Joseph Chilton Pearce's *cosmic egg* and the more recent *paradigm*. I shall use the simple term *worldview*, meaning the underlying assumptions, vocabulary, and framework upon which we base our thinking, feeling, and behavior in our life.

The world that we trustingly view as our reality is actually much more like a methodically induced trance in which we have little choice. (See Socrates' classic Allegory of the Cave in Plato's *Republic* for one of the earliest and most cogent dramatizations of this very point.) At the beginning of our individual lives, we seem to have little choice regarding the content and acquisition of a worldview. We are born into a society that has its own unique, generalized yet particularized worldview called its *culture*, which the society has developed to insure both its own and its members' survival.

Although culture is dynamic and changing over time, it can appear quite static when viewed in the short term, rather like a freeze-frame view. Society and its culture do change on the basis of what is discovered to be most valuable for their survival at any given time and under any given conditions. However, there is a highly conservative tendency that operates in a society, its members, and its culture. The society/culture can be viewed as an organism of great bulk that is quite single-minded, rather like a dinosaur. Its single-mindedness with regard to survival gives it a small brain, considering its bulk. Consequently, as conditions change, it will exhibit an inertia in its tendency to respond in the old "tried and true" ways that may be wholly inappropriate to the new situation.

A very recent example of the foregoing is our society's response to what it perceived as a "drug problem," to which it reacted quite unimaginatively with a "war on drugs"—nearly identical to the failed earlier "prohibition" policy on liquor, and with very similar results. (For an encouraging contrast, unequalled in its virtue, consider our nation's post–World War II Marshall Plan, as compared to the customary pillaging, subjugation, and vengefulness practiced by previous war victors.) Thus, societies and individuals, with fairly rare exceptions, tend to react to new challenges as though they were the old, familiar ones. It is easy to see why any society/culture, viewed in the short term, exhibits inconsistencies and contradictions that can manifest in so many ways, ranging from the humorous to the destructive.

Now, let us turn our attention to how the individual acquires culture and interactively, through experience, molds it into his/her worldview. This process is referred to by cultural anthropologists as *enculturation*, and it is every society's primary function.

Enculturation is basically a conditioning and reinforcing process, which includes the sanctions employed to enforce it; it is the means through which each individual can learn to survive in that society. Enculturation is accomplished through a variety of agents and agencies of the society, beginning with the mother or mother-surrogate and expanding to the whole family, however constituted. This is continued by other agencies, such as the neighborhood, peers, school, employer; social, religious, military, and political organizations; as well as other subsocieties, such as clubs and various associations. Every society employs such agencies or their counterparts and uses sanctions of varying severity to condition and reinforce the enculturation in its individual members. (For those who wish a more detailed inquiry into the foregoing, consult any basic text in cultural anthropology and in the psychology of learning, two fields whose elements are assumed to be familiar to the reader in order to help keep this work from unnecessarily becoming a tome.)

Central to the *enculturation process* is the conveyance to the individual of the primacy and importance of that society's single-mindedness; namely, that survival comes first. Although obviously true—that is, if one does not survive, nothing else is possible—both the society and the individual tend to conclude that survival is the *whole* point of living; as we shall see, that is clearly not the case. This is an understandable, but perilous, error. In other words, recognizing that something—such as survival—is necessary does not mean it is also sufficient; it is human mental laziness or ignorance that construes the necessary as also sufficient.

Here it would be well to look at survival more closely. At the first, most basic level is *subsistence survival*, which means satisfying the elemental needs or drives, such as those involving hunger, thirst, touch, sex, and shelter/protection. At this level there may also appear some of the basic learned technologies and strategies, inflowing from the next level, such as using the spear, drawing water from a well, cooking, tracking, trapping, and hunting in parties. Beyond subsistence survival, at the next level, is what I call *successful survival*, which entails the continued and assured satisfying of the elemental needs, as well as the many conditioned or enculturated desires that are based on or arise out of the elemental needs or the means developed to satisfy them. The enculturation process and the activities of larger societies are well under way at this second level.

Successful survival probably arose with the emergence of our earliest continuing cooperative efforts, such as the clan and the tribe (which grew out of successful hunting and gathering parties), and the later development of agriculture and the plow. In time, successful techniques for satisfying the elemental needs, along with various magical rituals (magical belief and thinking being a primitive and noteworthy precursor of and an attempt at conceiving of causality), came to be transferred from member to member, from parent to offspring. These techniques became conditioned as desires based upon satisfying the elemental needs, and then new desires based upon these successes developed into what I call derivative desires. This process of derivative desires continues down to this day to the point where it is difficult to discern the basic need or prior desire from which a current desire is derived.

For example, fashion and the desire to be fashionable arise rather indirectly out of the elemental needs to be clothed for shelter/protection and to attract a sex partner. However, these elemental needs almost cease to be recognizable in today's fashion industry, which seems to be based more on derivative desires for display, aesthetics, and conspicuous consumption, not to mention envy and greed. The fashion industry is integrated into our economy, which is a market system originally devised to assure the continued satisfying of elemental needs. This example illustrates how satisfying elemental needs, their derivative desires, and subsequent derivative desires can generate such varied entire institutions as the market system and the fashion industry.

Thus, successful survival goes beyond, while also subsuming, subsistence survival, evolving into the process of satisfying conditioned desires that can be traced back to the elemental needs and their derivative desires. The elemental needs are still operating, but practically cease to be recognizable after their incorporation into subsequent derivative desires.

In the transition from the subsistence survival level to the successful survival level, a unique evolutionary transformation occurred in human beings, which probably coincided with another unique development, namely language-acquisition ability, the prerequisite to structured, intentional thought. The very attempt by a human being to assure continued survival assumes the sense of continuity of that being, which requires the ability to conceive of an entity that survives and continues. Thus arose the sense of self, or ego—namely, that which continues beyond the immediate now. Of course, conceptualizing a continuing self requires language and mind, and that is why these two developments in human evolution emerged simultaneously in the transition of our species from subsistence survival to successful survival.

With the emergence of language and mind and a sense of self, there also arose the sense of not-self (beyond the strictly biological sense) and, consequently, the need for identity. The need then emerged for cooperation to assure continued survival more effectively. It is quite probable that the warning cry, oft-cited as the precursor to language, was more likely the precursor to the intentional cooperation so necessary to the development of society from the hunting and gathering group to the clan and family grouping, to the tribe, to the nation-state of more recent civilizations.

The transition from subsistence survival to the phase of continuing, assured, successful survival is based upon the attainment of a height in human cooperation—a common language, which is much more than words or utterances. A language, only spoken at first but much later written, is based upon a *shared world or reality*—a worldview, however individualized it may be from person to person.

Along with a common language, a successful society also develops shared technologies, such as gathering, mining, hunting, and farming. Religious techniques and devices, as well as steam engines, assembly lines, and computers, for example, are among the various apparatuses and implements employed by society and its members in the belief that they will assure continued survival. As an aid to memory and for the purposes of enculturation, these technologies become institutionalized and ritualized in schools, churches, temples, factories, and offices. This reflects a very human harmonizing/aesthetic impetus that emerges and eventuates in morality, religion, poetry, history, philosophy, and all the arts. On a large enough and continuing scale, this is what we call civilization, which we consider the summit of human achievement, even though we continue to see evidence all about us that we have so far to go.

Such shortcomings have resulted in two seemingly opposing tendencies in regard to prescriptions that we should follow to attain whatever promised land is being proffered and urged upon us. One would have us revert to or embrace some former reliable way, golden age, or magical religion; the other would have us march forward to a brave new world based on the latest "sociospiritual psychology." In either case, the direction that we are exhorted to follow is a corporate way based primarily on a *group* allegiance. Of course, this is quite understandable since the corporate way is the way that has always worked for successful survival and has led to civilization. What we fail to see are the limits of this corporate way.

As important and necessary as successful survival has been for humanity, certain values and derivatives flow from it that become the very *impediments* to our continued evolution and unfoldment of who we really are. As we will learn more fully later, each of us is here to discover and explore our *Areté* (ar'-i-tay'), which is the difficult-to-translate ancient Greek term for our unique, individual fullness, or excellence. Our failure in attaining this can be traced directly to the very habits, skills, and achievements that empower us for successful survival but that paradoxically can also work as impediments to our going beyond successful survival and reaching what I shall be calling the *Life of Fullness*. In other words, our coveted strengths at one level come to be our weaknesses at the next level, the stumbling blocks to our evolving fullness.

If this theme seems familiar, we can trace it back to those remarkable ancient Greeks who gave us the form of the *tragedy*. Unlike the modern degenerative meanings of this term, the essence of Greek tragedy involved a protagonist whose downfall proceeded with karmic inevitability due to a flaw based on what was considered to be strength or an outstanding, heroic quality. Those early Greeks perceptively called that flaw *hubris*, which is best translated as overweening pride. Is this not our own modern human condition? Both as a society and thus, derivatively, as individuals, we have developed, have available, and take great pride in the technologies, institutions, and other skills and resources that should, we imagine, lead to a golden age; but we find ourselves hopelessly inept at achieving it. Has this not even been the perennial theme of so much of our serious literature, both fiction and nonfiction? The greater our efforts, both individually and societally, to achieve this golden age or fulfillment, the greater does our failure manifest by achieving more nearly the opposite or some degeneracy of what we intended. Examples of this abound in our society: welfare, unemployment and workers' compensation, foreign aid, political and tax reform, and the allocation of more money to schools, minorities, prisons, and medical care. Of course, people can see this phenomenon working in their own individual lives just as clearly. What else is this but the *Tragic Life*?

Our *Areté*, or fullness, cannot be approached using the entirely inappropriate, lower-order successful survival categories and skills. Although we need these skills and abilities for our continued, assured survival, we need also to become aware of the extent to which they can be impediments to the Life of Fullness. This awareness must precede the "going beyond," or *Transcendence*, which is necessary to our evolutionary destiny. Otherwise, we are doomed to the limiting pridefulness of the Tragic Life, which becomes our lot when we cannot see beyond successful survival and its derivative values and manifestations.

This Tragic Life is at the heart of the continuing, nearly universal appeal of our myriad fear- and hope-based magical religions. (As we shall soon see, fear and hope conditioning arise out of and are fundamental to the enculturation process, as well as being the twin foundations of religions.) The Tragic Life makes understandable the widespread belief in so many religious dogmas, especially, for example, original sin. When we cannot go beyond successful survival, we are tempted—individually and collectively—to believe the fault is constitutional, that is, a birth defect of enormous and universal extent. (Whether this is believed literally or figuratively makes little difference in its effects.) That this belief also aids the purpose of social control is not lost on those who govern and thus virtually insures its pervasive incorporation into the enculturation process. As we shall see later, our only and enormous sin originates in the enculturation, and it is by the most sloppy, lazy, or expedient thinking that it can be considered original in the sense of innate.

In such a manner do people conclude that this is a problem to be understood and resolved by simply projecting an evil nature within. A quite different approach is taken by many other peoples and their religions. Instead of seeing an evil nature within, at, or before birth, they project the problem outward and after birth. In this schema, the errors and evil acts of a people accumulate in the world to the point of great imbalance, so a great, collective, world-renewal effort or ceremony is required, usually with a sacrifice of some kind or the creation of a scapegoat. (The roots of war-waging may even be found in such a view.) Thus the slate is wiped clean and the world is back in balance. In the first schema, the individual is required to confess and atone and thus wipe the slate clean. In both schemas, the solution is always temporary and must be repeated continuously, thus conferring great power on those in control, whether secular or sacerdotal.

Although religion evolved as a manifestation of successful survival and thus is not capable of taking the individual beyond it to the Life of Fullness, religion continues to be confused with the spiritual, or that realm or dimension which transcends successful survival. The evolution of religions has been well documented by various scholars, especially by cultural anthropologists and historians. The roots of these religions appeared in quite rudimentary masculine forms (for example, the use of certain animal parts in rituals, as well as phallic symbols) in our earliest hunting and gathering stage and then, by contrast, virtually flowering (for example, the earth mother and fertility rites) during our subsequent agricultural phase, a considerable leap in our species' efforts at assuring continued survival.

Agriculture made possible the more stable and increasingly territorial society, complete with all of the institutions that soon developed to insure that stability and territoriality, especially the legal, religious, and military establishments that both coerced individuals to conform and gave them the identity and sense of belonging necessary to any corporate effort. It was during this stage that many of our widespread current "world" religions erupted; often attributed to great teachers, supposedly based on their lives, but actually organized and developed upon the subsequent legends and caricatures that are the hallmarks of human communication through time. Such legends and caricatures are always selected to insure the hegemony of those in power at the time. Fortunately for the survival of these religions, reformations did occur at transition points in response to challenges and rapidly changing conditions.

In the Religious Era, or consciousness, religion serves the survival function of binding together people who view themselves as separate from one another, thus serving the societal needs for cohesion, stability, and control. In the Post-religious Era, or consciousness, as we shall see later, religion is transcended by those mutants, so very few at first, who become aware of the spiritual truth of our *Oneness*.

The term *religion* has its roots in the Latin *religio*, meaning "to bind together," a binding which can be seen as necessary only if the elements, the people, to be bound are first conceived of as separate from one another. Such a concept of separateness arises from the sense of self and the consequent sense of not-self that developed during the transition from subsistence survival to successful survival we discussed earlier. As we will see later, there is an impetus within us that seeks an ultimate union. We shall also see that such a union continually eludes us when it is attempted within the Life of Survival mode, the mode in which religion functions and flourishes and where it offers us *religio*, or the illusory binding together of apparently separate selves to one another and to God, thus serving as a counterfeit substitute for our impetus to an ultimate union.

This sense of separateness pervades the entirety of our existence in the world and has become the foundation of our worldview since the rise of what we call civilization. It is also the seed of the destruction of that civilization. Over the last three to four millennia, many wise men and women, sages, prophets, and teachers have tried to call attention to this disaster in the making and to the need for an inward reform, a change of worldview. This can be seen as a new order of warning cry at the societal level. The warning cries, uttered by these spiritual sentinels (for example, Gautama, Socrates, Jesus) are steeped in their respective cultures. They bear the stamp of time and place peculiar to their societies, employing the vocabulary and categories of their cultures. They also point beyond such limits to a spiritual realm that transcends the narrow contemporary focus of the Life of Survival, however it may be expressed in their society and time. What is sad and tragic is the reaction to such warning cries by both individuals and societies. Almost invariably, these warning cries are interpreted as threats to the dominant religion or society or some other aspect of the Life of Survival.

Well-meaning but misguided followers and so-called disciples who have misunderstood soon begin the process of developing legends and caricatures of the spiritual sentinels that are then incorporated into that society's subsequent Life of Survival—based religions. And the cycle—the appearance of these sentinels and the subsequent perverting of the inner meaning of these warning cries—continues unabated down through the centuries, even to this day.

Occasionally, however, individuals will become aware of these warning cries and make some attempt to respond. Such a response requires, as we shall see, the great courage to leap beyond the limits of the Life of Survival mode which has brought them to the awareness of the Tragic Life, the inevitable outcome of a life based solely on the criteria and worldview of successful survival.

Nevertheless, as we discussed earlier, successful survival is necessary, though not sufficient, for our continuing evolution toward the Life of Fullness. The journey that is the Life of Survival must be accomplished first, and successfully. Attaining that is what I shall call the *First Journey*. Then, such individuals must consider themselves successful survivors in that society. For this, there are no so-called objective criteria, such as wealth, title, or status. One may be a millionaire, a professional, or a craftsperson, have raised a splendid family, be a fine artist, or be otherwise accomplished and thus consider oneself a successful survivor. But we also know that many such achieving persons do not see themselves as successful survivors.

Why must this First Journey be accomplished successfully? The main reason is that there is a *Second Journey*, which is the adventure toward our *Areté* and which requires the strength and confidence derived from seeing oneself as successful on the First Journey. Neither strength nor confidence can be taught; they are by-products of the experience of successful survival. That is the initial requirement for a candidate for the Second Journey, and there are others.

The second requirement is more difficult to characterize. Simply put, one must have made various attempts at finding the meaning of life or spiritual fulfillment or developing one's human potential, only to be thwarted eventually by discovering the limits of whatever approach or way is being followed. These attempts have to be made not just for their own sake, but for what they reveal as prompting them. And this prompting or impetus I call the *Yearning*. You will note that the Yearning is not here followed by a preposition and an object, for there is no object for it in our experience, nor can there be. (For those of you with an existential or an academically philosophical bent, its realm is ontological.) Although the Yearning is innate and like a brilliance, our awareness of it becomes dimmer as we grow up, that is, become enculturated. This is not the result of some dark conspiracy by society; it is well intentioned and inevitable. You see, since society and the enculturation process are competent only in what matters to our Life of Survival, as we become enculturated, the Yearning is completely ignored because it has no survival value.

The Yearning is of our very nature. It is our awareness of it that dims, not the Yearning itself. There is a wonderful analogy for this. The Yearning is like a brilliant circle of light within us with which we are born. Each day of enculturation is like adding a layer of gauze over that circle of light. By the time we are adults, what started out as brilliant has become very obscured. In fact, when most people look within, all they come to see resembles a black hole.

Although our awareness of the Yearning dims, it is still there, generally unable to break through the grid of our enculturated worldview, which has no categories or vocabulary for its expression. However, on rare unguarded occasions, the Yearning does break through that grid to our consciousness as the equivalent of a whisper or a glimpse. For those who would like to explore this process in greater detail, I can think of no better characterization than that presented by Joseph Chilton Pearce in his book *The Crack in the Cosmic Egg*, a modern landmark in spiritual literature. For Pearce, the enculturated worldview is our Cosmic Egg, and he deftly explores how our awareness of the "crack" comes about, and what its consequences for us can be.

Thus, this Yearning beckons us in our search for meaning, spiritual fulfillment, or whatever we may call this Second Journey. What we perceive as glimpses associated with it are assurances that there *is* another realm or dimension to explore. However, the value of these glimpses for us is not in their recapturing; it is what they assure us of that is of value. (Many cults, fads, and other dead ends have been founded on such glimpses and the subsequent attempts at their recapture.)

The third requirement is the sequel to the second. Prompted by the Yearning, we search "lo here, lo there," almost endlessly, assured by our glimpses that there is another realm in which our real being is. Alas, we do not find it, and for a very simple reason. The way into the Second Journey cannot be found using the principles, concepts, vocabulary, and approaches we have mastered in becoming successful survivors. But these are all we have at that point. Hence, such searches are doomed.

The great majority of these searchers give up this quest, although they do not usually see it that way. What often happens is that they settle for a predigested counterfeit of the Second Journey, which is not a journey but actually a comfortable resting place where there are others in the same boat, and this takes on all of the aspects of what has come to be called the "lifeboat experience." More on this later.

A very small minority does not give in to this comforting way. They do not settle for any counterfeit. Yet the search nevertheless seems doomed. This is most discouraging, and although these individuals will, from time to time, have had bottoming-out experiences occasioned by some loss or disappointment of a hoped-for goal or expectation, these are nothing compared to the ultimate bottoming-out experience. This is the direct result of their discovering the limits of the ways of searching based on the application of successful survival skills and concepts. The repeated discoveries of these limits, and the consequent bottoming-out in each case, lead to an *awareness of their despair*. This is the third prerequisite for starting the Second Journey.

The next requirement is simple, but by no means easy. This awareness of our despair and its determinants, together with our prior assurance that there is another realm or dimension to be explored, should lead to a dramatic 180° turn. This would be a turn *away* from our exclusive reliance upon a clearly bankrupt process and *toward* an unknown realm. This is a very difficult move and is accomplished only rarely. I could get fancy here and describe this difficulty psychologically, but it is succinctly summed up in that old Jamaican expression: "We stick to the evil we know." Here, the evil we know consists of successful-for-survival conditionings that we must come to realize are inappropriate for the Second Journey. So, the fourth requirement entails the will to turn away from this reliance upon the bankrupt known and toward the unknown realm in the spirit of an explorer.

This turning toward the unknown realm requires great courage because what is being attempted here is nothing less than *Transcendence*, which we will explore more fully later but which means, briefly, going beyond the limits of what we know or can do. Doing this puts us right in what I call *No-man's-land* because we have left *Man's-land*, that is, the familiar, controllable world that we have built up and relied upon throughout our First Journey. In No-man's-land there are no equivalents of signposts, familiar landmarks, or reference points, and that is fearsome to us. Many have entered this transitional realm without guidance only to suffer the direst consequences: either madness or suicide. An example of each that comes to mind is the philosopher Friedrich Nietzsche and the poet Sylvia Plath, both of whom persistently attempted to go unguided beyond their enculturated tether.

This No-man's-land must be entered and traversed, and that requires the aid of a guide. What is a guide in any endeavor? Quite simply, it is someone who has been there and is willing to show others. But why is a guide necessary? Remember that here we are leaving Man's-land where we have been conditioned to seek the familiar, the predictable, or the controllable, but the unfamiliar, unpredictable, or uncontrollable is tolerated ever so briefly in our lives. Yet, these are pervasive features of No-man's-land, which does not submit to our initial, automatic efforts to make it familiar and controllable. Herein lies a seemingly inescapable dilemma. Our initial, automatic attempts to make No-man's-land familiar and controllable simply land us back in Man's-land. But not making these attempts soon becomes intolerable, and unguided persistence in this manner leads eventually, even if protractedly, to madness or suicide. Are we doomed? No—this is why the guide is so necessary. There is no way to make No-man's-land familiar and controllable, but the guide can help one learn what is needed there: *Learning to live moment by moment in this realm whose substance and process will neither become familiar in the usual sense nor be controllable.*

That is the challenge of this journey into the realm of our Yearning. This is a twofold challenge. First, we must become familiar with our inner ecology in order to discover the source and ways that pollute us internally. This will be the task of the first half of this book. Second, we need to explore the process of correcting that pollution which so hinders our taking the Second Journey. And that will be presented in the second half of the book.

We are destined for this process of evolution in consciousness. However, this is a unique challenge, in that it must be chosen by individual will. The choice is ours once we become aware of the Yearning. Ignoring the Yearning leads only to the easy, wasteful life of ennui that we see all around us, most pitifully in the elderly who have waited too long. The simple, generative, adventurous way of this challenge is to embark on the Second Journey.

This book is for beginners—that is, for those who are truly ready to begin a journey—and the foregoing has been an attempt to provide a simple overview of the prerequisites to, as well as some basic features of, the transformational Second Journey. This is a unique journey in an unaccustomed dimension, often referred to as spiritual, the inward way, or the way of the mystic. You will soon see that the mystic is actually the most practical person alive. Do not be misled by any preconceptions: this is not a retreat or a way out. It is the way *in*—to a reality that reveals the conventional view of reality as the barrier or stumbling block it often is to the realm of our evolving higher consciousness.

2

CAVEATS AND PREFATORY REMARKS

A recurring frustration of trying to present this vision of our higher consciousness is that we have to start by using our current worldview categories and vocabulary. Remember that this worldview and vocabulary have developed to deal entirely with what I refer to as the Life of Survival. The Life of Fullness, or higher consciousness, does not submit to these categories and vocabulary; yet, we must use these to build a necessary bridge. We have a dual task here. One is to become aware of the shortcomings and even attempt to clean up some of the mess of invalid assumptions, inferences, and other misconceptions of our current worldview that limit its usefulness even for the purpose of bridging. The other task is to become aware of the thinking and work that is being done at the edges or on the frontiers of our collective worldview that are leading to generative new paradigms that can highlight and help us break through the limits of our current worldview. Each of these tasks would undoubtedly entail the other, and they can help us in building the bridging concepts and framework we will need for the Second Journey. This dual task must be undertaken by each person individually and must have been initiated prior to this book journey. Thus, one would become increasingly aware of the limits inherent in our current worldview, and this awareness would serve as the basis of the caveats needed to explore beyond such limits. A review of salient elements from various fields, such as general semantics, linguistics, developmental psychology, physics, and philosophy would be helpful at this point, but we must limit this to just a few reminders.

First, let us note that the birth of a new paradigm is always necessarily expressed in terms of the existing paradigm, until a base of committed adherents has arisen who can generate the requisite new framework and vocabulary as the result of thinking, feeling, and acting upon the new. Consider, for example, Galileo's observations and theories, the Roman Catholic Church's reaction, and the world's eventual adoption of his views. So, we cannot expect a familiar, ready-made framework or vocabulary awaiting us in the work ahead.

Second, we need to remember that a fundamental of learning something new entails relating it to something already known. This principle applies not only to individual learning but also to language in general; this is what I call the *metaphoric* principle or process. In other words, language—both in the individual and in general—grows metaphorically. This is fine for our Life of Survival, where the causal, logical, and other epistemological principles of our worldview apply fairly consistently. However, these do not apply when we embark on the Second Journey, when we must be most aware of our use of metaphor. And yet, we must talk about this Second Journey, at least to introduce it and, in a sense, to build a bridge to it. The words and concepts I use here will be *pointing* to a realm beyond any of our Life of Survival experiences, categories, or worldviews. Rather than press further into epistemological discourse here, let me sum up by means of that elegant Zen aphorism: "Don't mistake the pointing finger for the moon."

Further, we will be using familiar words and concepts in rather unfamiliar ways, and this requires a great deal of patience and openness. Whenever such a familiar word or concept is used, remember that it is being used to point beyond the familiar in a direction that bears exploring. Thus, we must not be hasty in attaching any conclusive meaning, but rather must keep the boundaries very open during the exploration. For example, thus far I have introduced a number of words and concepts, and there are numerous others, to characterize the overall realm we will be exploring: Life of the Spirit, Life of Fullness, spiritual, the Inward Way, the way of the mystic, the Second Journey, higher realm or dimension, higher consciousness, the God beyond God, the Godhead, the Kingdom of Heaven, the Way, Enlightenment, the Ultimate, the Absolute, not to mention the many useful and helpful non-English terms (for example, the Tao, Nirvana) that have found their way into our vocabulary. All of these terms and many others merely point at different facets of this realm beyond for our exploration.

What I am trying to convey here is that we have all sorts of habits of thought that are the result of our enculturation (for an elaboration of this point, see the works of Benjamin Whorf and Edward Sapir, as well as Ludwig Wittgenstein's later work, for example). These habits are necessary and useful in our Life of Survival, but they can be impediments to the Second Journey. Since we must continue surviving, there is no doing without them, but we can become aware of them and their limits. That is, we need to become aware of the limits of discursive thought and its vehicle, our language, in this higher realm of consciousness.

By way of illustration, let us look at some terms that are often used in describing the Life of Fullness, namely *beyond*, *within*, *higher*, and *deeper*. These words, first of all, show us how spatially based our language is: literally, they describe spatial characteristics. However, we also use these words figuratively to describe nonspatial qualities, such as importance, intensity, or priority, with which we are all familiar. We do so because we can refer them to experiences that we have had in common even though these experiences have no spatial referents.

Now what happens when we use these terms in discussing the Life of Fullness? We readily admit that we are not using the terms literally. However, all too often a confusion arises when we think we are using them figuratively. To do so would require that they refer to experiences we have in common, and that is clearly not the case. The Life of Fullness is not based on experiences as we ordinarily use that term. Experiences occur in the spatiotemporal matrix, and the Life of Fullness, while subsuming it, transcends that matrix. Hence, when we use such terms as *beyond, within, higher, deeper,* and others to describe the Life of Fullness, we are pointing beyond the spatiotemporal matrix of our language and experiences to a higher realm of consciousness.

So even though we quite readily admit the limits of using terms literally in our language, we are not usually so aware of the limits of the figurative use of terms. We have seen that terms can have a transliteral sense that we call figurative, which employs the familiar metaphoric transformer that relates the new to the shared known. And now, we see that terms can have a transfigurative sense for which we have no name, except perhaps *transcendent.* This transcendent sense of language requires that we resist our usual inclinations to arrive at closures, conclusions, and generalizations of meaning. These meanings must be left quite tentative and open to further illumination. That is why we must embark on this Second Journey as intrepid-yet-patient explorers open to whatever we encounter, knowing that what we encounter will not fit the Procrustean bed of our language and thoughts—that is, our worldview.

Our language has another fundamental problem that has continually misled us at all levels of our lives, whether in philosophy, politics, or simple everyday matters. This difficulty is due to the basic structure of our language, in which we divide our reality into nouns and verbs. We cannot make a single statement in and about our world without dividing it into a noun and a verb, or an agent and an action. "Well, what is the problem with that?" one might well ask. Our lack of awareness of this problem just shows how deeply immersed we are in it. In fact, it is only in this last century that we have become more aware of it, thanks primarily to the many theoretical physicists and the few philosophers who have succinctly pointed out this fundamental misconception. Simply put, they see reality in terms of dynamic processes and continuity rather than as discontinuous entities acting on or creating events in the world, which is the way our language is structured.

Remember, it used to be thought that, even if all else were process, there were irreducible entities in our world; that is, atoms. First, these were further reduced to subatomic particles, such as protons, neutrons, electrons, and so on. Then, even these came to be seen as various manifestations of not matter, but more fundamental dynamic processes, such as energy or forces. So, to many theoretical physicists and philosophers, all is process. What we used to see as entities—whether electron, table, person, star, cosmos, or God, for example—are more meaningfully and accurately seen as dynamic, continuous processes.

However, this fundamental change has not "trickled down" or diffused very far from the theoretical physicists and philosophers, such as Einstein, Heisenberg, and Whitehead, and neither has our language developed to reflect this revelation. It is most instructive to reflect on how we (in the West) first became aware of this difficulty and how it was resolved. To do this, we must go back to the seventeenth century, to the early stages of the development of modern physics. During that period, it had become apparent that our language (that is, any of the Indo-European family of languages) was woefully inadequate to the task of describing dynamic processes in nature. The awareness of this limit led to a most remarkable invention: an artificial language. This was accomplished simultaneously by two men, Leibniz and Newton, and that artificial language has come to be known as the calculus.

The very existence of the calculus points out that great deficiency in our language regarding the description of dynamic and/or continuous processes. Whenever we attempt to do so, we end up creating the most stilted and misleading constructs or fictions. As an example, let us look at a very commonplace expression: "It is raining." We are observing a dynamic process, but we are forced by our language to use both a noun and a verb. Pray tell, what is the *it* that is raining? We had to create a fictional *it*!

Actually, every time we use a noun, we are creating a fiction. Whether the noun is *pebble, table, person, William, society, world,* or *cosmos*, we now know that these are each dynamic processes that are continuous with all of reality. However, our language causes us to treat each as a discrete, fixed, and unchanging entity, which is certainly a fiction.

What, then, can be done about such a serious shortcoming in our language and worldview? In our ordinary, everyday practice, not much. However, whenever we go beyond the ordinary and the everyday, we must be keenly aware of this fundamental shortcoming at all times. Otherwise, we can be terribly misled when we use such nouns as *humanity, soul, cosmos, love, God,* and so on. We must keep in mind that in each such case, we are talking or thinking about a dynamic process that is continuous with all of reality, but we are using such terms tentatively, and primarily for *our* convenience, in order to go beyond them; that is, to transcend the language.

In the Life of Survival, we will, from time to time, find ourselves at the limits of an endeavor or way of thinking, whether it is a course of action we have chosen and taken or a belief or philosophical position we have assumed and lived by. Our usual reaction to discovering such limits is to commit a fundamental error: we tend to redouble our original efforts; that is, we simply amplify our conditioning in the same direction and consequently encounter the same intractable limits. The root of this error lies in our being conditioned to seek the familiar and predictable, which may work fine in the Life of Survival, but which impedes us on the Second Journey.

For the Life of Fullness, there is a need to transcend these limits, and the first step is to recognize them as limits of our conditioned Life of Survival. The willingness to do this opens us up to the discontinuities of the realm of the unknown. And it is just such discontinuities in our lives that we have to learn to welcome rather than avoid. Examples of these in our Life of Survival are the loss of a job or promotion, separation or divorce, and other changes in valued relationships, as well as any other events that we interpret as setbacks or failures. Such manifestations of discontinuity involve the disappointment of our goals and purposes, whereas continuity involves the realization of our goals and purposes, even if unexpected at the time. Continuity is what we have been conditioned to seek in our lives, and as valuable as that is in our Life of Survival, it can be an impediment to Transcendence. Discontinuity *can* lead to both discovering and transcending the limits. There is no transcending without discontinuity. (This will be elaborated upon later.)

The foregoing caveats and prefatory remarks are intended as warnings to the reader of some of the more basic impediments to embarking on the Second Journey. There are others which will be elucidated contextually as we proceed. However, it should be noted that in each case of a caveat, my remarks do provide a way around the impediments if one can maintain openness and patience.

3

THE FIRST JOURNEY:
THE LIFE OF SURVIVAL

*I*n order to see how one arrives at the embarkation point of the Second Journey, we must explore in greater detail the First Journey, which leads some of us to the stage of radical questioning, existential angst, or dark night of the soul, and questing. Going beyond this stage, however, requires having a successful First Journey. This First Journey consists primarily of the Life of Survival, which is best characterized by and accomplished through the process called enculturation.

It is generally accepted that enculturation may begin for the individual at least as early as conception, and there may be arguments for pushing it back to the sperm and ovum stage since they, too, are influenced by an environment. However, for our purposes, it is important only to be aware that enculturation begins quite early, preverbally. Remember, it is the process by which a given society, through its various agencies, transmits to and conditions in individuals its culture. This culture consists of all of the ways that the society has deemed to be successful adaptations to what it considers to be its world.

The earliest stage of enculturation is dominated by the family, especially the mother or mother surrogate, well expressed as "learning at your mother's knee"—although soon enough other members of the family become involved. The family's function remains the same, but it may be constituted variously depending upon the particular society, situation, and time involved. As the child grows, other agencies of enculturation come into play: neighbors, peers, religions, schools, employers, the state and its agencies, the mass media, as well as other subsocieties, such as associations and clubs. The primary process by which enculturation proceeds with respect to the individual is called conditioning, including the subsequent and necessary reinforcement, accompanied by sanctions and rewards. A great deal is understood about conditioning and reinforcement, but there are some fundamentals of the sanctioning and rewarding process that require further exploration.

Although the earliest enculturation involves primarily sensory/motor and then behavioral elements, much of the conditioning soon becomes more abstracted (that is, mental in nature) with the advent of language acquisition. However, keep in mind that all subsequent conditioning builds on the foundation of that earliest sensory/motor conditioning, which also serves as the basic framework of what we conventionally call our awareness. Along with the sensory/motor, behavioral, and mental conditioning, there is the equally important, and quite elemental, affective conditioning.

Affective conditioning has two sides to it. The *light side* includes caring, acceptance, understanding, cuddling, and stroking— often denoted as "love"—which, once experienced, we all tend to seek throughout our lives in various forms. Far less understood is the *dark side*, which we also tend to seek throughout our lives in various forms and which, along with the light side, parallels our behavioral and mental conditioning. This dark side consists mainly of two learned processes which are usually mistakenly considered inborn: the *Fear process* and the *Hope process*.

Yes, fear is learned as a process necessary for survival. It should not be confused with the state of being startled, which is an inborn reaction to sudden, new, or unexpected stimuli. It is what we do after being startled that is learned, and that conditioning is quite elaborate and continually reinforced. Although fear may elicit emotions and have some behavioral precursors, its core is primarily a *mental* process. A moment's reflection on the process will bear this out. An instance begins with a stimulus—for example, a dog barking suddenly and nearby—which startles us from slightly to intensely, and then we mentally project an undesirable outcome, such as the dog biting us and the attendant pain, which we react to mentally with avoidance or repulsion.

Any object or situation can be the occasion of fear, but we must not confuse the Fear process with any of its myriad potential objects. Also, note that the event or situation that causes the startle, as well as the reaction of avoidance or repulsion, actually takes place in the present. And although the mental projection also occurs in the present, it actually involves the imaginary creation of future events. It is this *mental imagining of what is not present* that is the core of the Fear process. We, in effect, delegate power over us to something imaginary and not in the here and now. (It is interesting to note here that this is practically the same process that is being touted these days by pop psychologists, spiritualists, and others as the "visualization" necessary to achieve a desired goal.)

How did we come to this? As individuals, we learned the Fear process starting "at our mother's knee," and that conditioning process was continued by all the other agencies of enculturation. It is considered necessary for our survival, which it is in the early stages of our development. Until we are capable of more abstract and generalized thinking, we need the vivid images of dire consequences when we do not do that which our society considers desirable for survival. Like our fear-based religions, which tend to keep us in the kindergarten of spiritual development, the Fear process continues unabated and is reinforced for all of our lives instead of being transcended.

From its simple beginnings as an enculturation tool, the Fear process soon becomes perverted. Soon enough, we no longer await the external stimulus, but we learn to generate these stimuli internally and react as though they were actually present. The reason for this perversion is quite simple and is to be found in the psychology of learning concept called habituation, which is the basis of all addiction, whether it is at the micro (cellular) or the macro (psychological or societal) level. The Fear process may start out as an occasional tool of the enculturation process but soon enough becomes pervasive and continual. During this conditioning, we become addicted to the Fear process so that, like any addict, when the stimulus is not present externally, we will seek it or even generate it internally in order to achieve the "kick" of our reaction to the stimulus (for example, horror books or films, bungee-jumping, and random worrying).

Since our consensual worldview incorporates not only a present but also a past and a future, it should not surprise us that we also have past and future versions of the Fear process. These are called guilt and anxiety. When the Fear process points to our *past*, it is called *guilt*. We ill-use our imagination to call up a remembered, painful past event that acts as the stimulus to which we react mostly internally, though often externally as well. Guilt is simply that form of the Fear process in which the stimulus is generated from what we claim as our past. The extreme form of this is called being guilt-ridden and can result in the opposite of healthy growth—stunting or near-paralysis.

An interesting manifestation of a widespread manipulative use of guilt occurs when people say or do something, usually intentionally and even calculatedly for their own benefit, to elicit sympathy or to induce some desired behavior. Although in the field of ethnic humor, this gambit has been attributed narrowly to the "Jewish (or Italian) mother," it is really quite rampant and recognizable in so many close relationships. It can occur as an intentionally manipulative ploy but often is also done out of habit, and with minimal awareness in many families and other small groups. It is also employed in larger groups to provoke some desired behavior and feelings, as in fund-raising, morale-building, as well as in religions and for any other group-cohesion purposes. For this phenomenon, I coined the term "guilting," as well as the verb "to guilt."

When the Fear process points to our *future*, we call it *anxiety*. Again, we ill-use our imagination to call up an anticipated painful event that acts as the stimulus to which we react mostly internally but also often externally. Anxiety is simply that form of the Fear process in which the stimulus is generated from what we claim as our future. The extreme form of this is called "anxiety-ridden" or free-floating anxiety, which can also result in the stunting or near-paralysis that is the opposite of healthy growth.

A useful image here is a metaphor I have used for many years, and that is the "worry organ." (Worry is used here simply as a synonym for anxiety.) The enculturation seems to develop in us a worry organ which, like the stomach, starts growling when it is not fed. So, we have to find its food, an anticipated painful event, and feed it to quell the growling. The worry organ can, of course, become a ravenous organ; remember what was said earlier about habituation and addiction, for that applies to both guilt and anxiety. (And yes, we also have a guilt organ, as well as a general fear organ, so all of this applies analogically to them, too.) What we barely grasp about this is that if the worry organ is not fed, being so ravenous and indiscriminate, it will soon begin to consume itself. But this requires a kind of cold-turkey approach for which there is little encouragement or teaching available. Worry is also often confused with genuine concern, especially when done by parents or a loved one, and consequently we can mistakenly come to regard it as a positive or constructive act.

Looking to the past or future can, of course, be instructive and growth-inducing, as when we learn from our errors or when we plan constructively for an impending occasion or project. However, this is not the case with guilt or anxiety. These other forms of the Fear process also function like addictions with the resultant pain, habituation requiring larger doses, and little or no constructive learning. Which of us has not known such a guilt- or anxiety-ridden person for whom this is disabling to some considerable extent?

The second half of the dark side of our affective conditioning is called the Hope process. Society must have learned a long time ago in our sociopsychological development that fear alone as an inducement is effective only in the short term; that in the long term it leads to apathy and near-paralysis, which do not have survival value. Yet, fear is an effective short-term conditioning tool and does thereby have survival value. Society had to find a way of continuing to use fear in a way that would not lead to the subsequent apathy and near-paralysis. Thus was born the Hope process that, when alloyed to the Fear process, provided in the individual a most powerful and continuing inducement to learn. (Note that alloys are often developed because they work more effectively than any of their constituents alone.)

The Hope process, like the Fear process, is also learned "at our mother's knee" and continued by family and all the other agencies of enculturation. In the Hope process, we have learned to use our imagination to project a desirable goal in the present or an outcome in the future. Again, in effect, we delegate power over us to something imaginary and not in the present. The contents or objects of the Hope process are varied and innumerable, generally conditioned in us by the various agencies of our society as part of the enculturation. Examples are high school or college graduation, a new car, marriage, a good job, a house, relationships, advancements, and even heaven.

The Hope process also starts out as an occasional, necessary, and desirable tool of enculturation, but through its continued use and resultant habituation, we soon become so addicted to it that we become "hope junkies" and have a hard time living in the present; in its extreme form, individuals may spend nearly all of their time in an imaginary, hoped-for world, which gets them classified as mentally ill.

The Fear process, including guilt and anxiety, and the Hope process are necessary in the enculturation process, as society is currently constituted, until we have become successful survivors. These illusory processes, like their exemplars, the boogeyman and fairy tales, need to be outgrown. It is interesting to note that, although we do outgrow the boogeyman and fairy tales as objects of the Fear and Hope processes, we do not learn to outgrow these processes themselves. Witness the widespread pandering to fear and hope in our society (and others similarly) in the ever-popular forms of horror books or films and soap operas, not to mention the entire fields of entertainment, advertising, propaganda, self-help psychology, and allied forms of motivational activities. Note the clever mixture of fear and hope in nearly every effective television commercial and political speech, not to mention television evangelists.

Those, and the myriad other fear- and hope-inducing activities available in our society, as well as their pervasive support by both our economy and the government, attest to the addictive nature of these processes which start out simply as the carrot and the stick of the enculturation process. They should function more like breast-feeding, something necessary and desirable in an early stage but to be outgrown and deemed unnecessary and undesirable as we mature. Failing to outgrow them results in our habituation, and consequent addiction, to the Fear and Hope processes in which can be found the roots of so much of what is currently called mental illness. What else, for example, is manic-depressive (*bipolar* is the currently fashionable term) but the oscillation between these two fundamental conditionings in people, alternating between the torpor of fear/anxiety and the elation of illusory hope? (Although it is not within the scope of this book, it would be a great service if some intrepid psychologist would venture beyond the present paradigms to explore this relationship between the Fear and Hope processes and what is called mental illness.)

Please remember that the enculturation process, like the birth process, is not bad or evil, but simply necessary in leading us toward successful survival and the accomplishment of the First Journey. (An excellent metaphor here is boot camp or basic training in the military.) The task then is not to deny or destroy it, which some so-called spiritual disciplines have advocated in part or in whole, but rather to transcend it. This is done by using the strength and confidence acquired as a by-product of successful survival to go beyond the limits of our ordinary existence—that is, of our behavioral, mental, and affective conditioning. Since society has not yet evolved beyond the Fear and Hope processes, it becomes incumbent upon rare individuals to be the mutants of this evolutionary step. Such transcending requires that we turn away from our sole reliance upon our Life of Survival conditionings and turn toward the Second Journey, which we will explore after we have delved into some little-known aspects of human nature.

The term *human nature* bears further inquiry because it is often confused with what should be called *human norms*. Human nature refers to what is of the nature or essence of being human. Human norms refer to what is observed in humans— that is, what is statistically or anecdotally normal in human beings; this is the domain of psychology, sociology, anthropology, linguistics, economics, political science, biology, and their offshoots. It is from such fields of study that we discover what is normal, and consequently what is deviant, in humans. In other words, the study of postenculturated humans is what yields human norms and what we consequently consider deviant.

What is considered deviant behavior or tendency falls into two categories that I call *misenculturation* and *malenculturation*, which are simply definitional terms. Each society has a set of goals and visions of what it considers successful enculturation. Behavior that does not contribute to this is considered deviant.

Malenculturation includes deviant behavior that is against the laws or codes of that society. Misenculturation encompasses deviant behavior that is considered undesirable or does not conform to the mores, but is not against the laws or codes of that society. What are termed misenculturation and malenculturation will vary not only from society to society but also from time to time.

In our society, this is quite evident in the study over time of such behaviors as homosexuality, public and private nudity, gender roles, and occupations. Homosexuality is a good example of behavior that was previously considered malenculturation but is now usually considered at most only misenculturation. The study of enculturation, misenculturation, and malenculturation are the domain of the psychological and social sciences, which study such human norms and their deviations. Although these fields and studies at their best can take us to the threshold of the domain of human nature, they are incompetent beyond that threshold.

The studies of postenculturated human norms and their deviations, such as in psychology and sociology, are based on unquestioned preenculturated human assumptions, and these studies can help take us to the threshold of transenculturated human nature. (An example of a preenculturated human assumption will be discussed shortly, and transenculturated human nature simply refers to our true human nature that transcends our enculturated Life of Survival and is what this book is all about.) The domain of human nature crosses that threshold and requires a different methodology based on a necessarily more speculative and philosophical approach. This involves the study of the preenculturated and transenculturated human, and these studies can be as rigorous and scientific (not scientistic, as is all too often the norm today, especially in the psychological and social sciences) as the study of nuclear physics.

In fact, books too numerous to cite (for example, Fritjof

Capra's *The Tao of Physics* and Gary Zukav's *The Dancing Wu Li Masters*) are drawing remarkable parallels between the study of theoretical physics and the study of preenculturated and trans-enculturated human nature. However, there is a tendency here to infer from such parallels that these fields are practically identical. (See Ken Wilber's *Eye to Eye* for an excellent exposition of this fallacy and of much more to whet the appetite of the intelligent inquirer.)

There is also a perverted use of the term *human nature* which is widespread in the vernacular of ordinary discourse. All too often, when describing an instance of enculturated behavior that exceeds the norm, such as in the seven "deadly sins," people will exclaim: "Well, that's human nature." Just because some humans exhibit a tendency to such enculturation-based behavior does not justify calling it human nature. We need to remember that attitudes and behavior, such as the so-called deadly sins, are actually extremes or perversions of healthy needs or expressions, (for example, gluttony or lust as extremes of hunger or sexuality, respectively). These would be better explained as the effects of habituation and subsequent addiction, which were discussed earlier.

Generally, the expression "Well, that's human nature" betrays a mental laziness or an unwillingness to explore the phenomenon in question more fully. We must reserve the term *human nature* for what is the *essence* of being human and not use it when we are simply describing either enculturated human norms or their related deviations. We must distinguish between enculturated human norms (and their deviations), which are the domain of the psychological and social sciences, and the preenculturated and transenculturated human nature, which are the domain of philosophy and the Life of Fullness, respectively.

Let us consider here an example of an unquestioned preenculturated human assumption that is widespread in the social, psychological, and biological sciences. The variables studied in such fields are assumed to fall into two basic categories, variously expressed as heredity/environment, nature/nurture, genetic/learned, or inborn/acquired. This two-category schema is so obviously a preenculturated human assumption; one rarely sees it questioned, except to favor one category over the other or occasionally to combine the two as a way out of a dilemma. Yet, this schema clearly begs to be challenged. For twenty-five years, I have advocated using a third category: the *Umbilicum process.* This is not an entity, but a dynamic, metabiological, transexperiential, communicative network process by means of which members of a species transmit and receive "learnings" to and from one another through and from (what I intentionally vaguely refer to as) the *Source.* I would also include interspecies and extraspecies communion and communication.

The Umbilicum process can be seen as nonlocal organizing fields that both transmit and receive information to and from our world of existence. (A superb introduction to the concept of nonlocality, as well as much else of great value, is to be found in Larry Dossey's *Recovering the Soul*; this book and Joseph Chilton Pearce's *Evolution's End* would be excellent as companion volumes for this work.) Without this third category, the Umbilicum process, it is impossible to account for such phenomena as revelation, the creative process in musical and other geniuses, or specieswide acquiring of skills, such as the nest-building habits of various bird species and the sudden specieswide behavioral adaptations that have been observed and reported. All of these occur without the normally requisite conditioning process, nor can they be explained via the "hard-wired" genetic process. (More on this, especially revelation, later. Those who would like to follow a contemporary scientist's revolutionary explorations of this third category are advised to look at Rupert Sheldrake's *A New Science* and *The Presence of the Past*, especially his concepts of "morphogenetic fields" and "morphic resonance," in which he creates a framework to explain how such "learnings" or "habits" may be transmitted and acquired without the normally antecedent conditioning process.)

To summarize, it is through the enculturation process that we can learn to survive successfully. It is through this process that so many of our human potentials, such as language acquisition and various sensory/motor/mental skills, are achieved. There are no objective criteria of successful survival, only the individual's own judgment, based on the by-products of the strength and confidence acquired therein. In addition to sensory/motor, behavioral, and mental conditioning, we also undergo affective conditioning, consisting of a light and a dark side. The light side includes what are conventionally called compassion, love, respect, consideration, and so on. The dark side—far less understood—consists mainly of the Fear process, including guilt and anxiety, and the Hope process.

The severe limits of enculturation can be seen in that it does not provide a way to mature beyond these Fear and Hope processes, which were so important in motivating our earlier conditionings. This results in a stunting or perversion of our human potential, as well as often even precluding what I have called successful survival, the prerequisite for embarking on the Second Journey. In our age, an example of such stunting and perversion would be the legion of nearly stereotypical, often unidimensional, "successful" businessmen, politicos, or professionals whose strivings in the Life of Survival are feverish and continue unabated to the point where such behavior can only be considered habituation and addiction.

4

QUESTING, YEARNING, AND THE UMBILICUM PROCESS

*T*here is a unique propensity in humans that I call the *Questing*, which is a nesting, hierarchical process (for an introduction to this concept, see Arthur Koestler's *The Ghost in the Machine* and *Janus*). The Questing begins at the first level of this hierarchical process, with the searching that we share with other species for the elemental survival needs, such as food, water, sex, and shelter/protection. This is the *first* or *subsistence survival* level. In humans, as these needs are sufficiently satisfied and as the limits of that level are discovered, the Questing transcends to the *second* or *creating the useful* level, finding expression in things like the wheel; in interrelated processes like customs, religions, morality, and laws; and in institutions, such as families, clans, tribes, and nations. As the second level of the Questing becomes more and more satisfied and its limits discovered, it can then be transcended to the next level in the quest for harmony or creating the aesthetically pleasing, including science, philosophy, theology, and other intellectual pursuits, as well as poetry, music, dance, architecture, and other arts. This is the *third* or *creating the harmonizing/aesthetic* level.

If we stopped at the second or creating the useful level, the most we could attain is successful survival. If, however, we satisfied the second level, became aware of its limits, and then transcended to the third or creating the harmonizing/aesthetic level, the best we could then attain is a well-decorated and pleasurable successful survival. Beyond this third hierarchical level is what is usually called the search or quest for meaning or, as I prefer, the quest for Fullness (or the spiritual, if you do not construe this term too narrowly or too parochially). I call this the *fourth* or *Life of Fullness* level, which we will explore in greater depth later, since it is at that level that we can discover and become aware of our Soul and its meaning.

To be fully human is to engage in this lifelong process of Questing, continuing from one hierarchical level to the next as the prior level becomes satisfied and its limits discovered. Settling for any level before the Life of Fullness will doom us to a rather stunted, despairing existence, no matter how externally full; witness especially the great majority of the elderly in our society, not to mention the wealthy and the famous, who simply become more adept at concealing their despair or disguising it with distractions and diversions.

With rare exception, organized religions manage to participate in satisfying only the second or, at most, reaching the third level of this hierarchy. However, in some of the lesser-known literature that religions preserve, as well as in accounts of the lives of mystics who have gone beyond the constraints of their religions, we find so many attempts, under many guises, to point to the fourth level of the Life of Fullness. This is clearly a natural evolution.

At the first or subsistence survival level of this Questing hierarchy, the object sought is invariably quite concrete, such as food, water, or a shelter/protection item. At the second or creating the useful level, much of our effort, individually and societally, is directed at first toward objects, such as tools, useful for assuring continued survival. At this and each successive level of this hierarchy, the object of the Questing becomes more abstract or abstractly based and less material or thing-based. This is quite apparent as we move from the first to the second level and from the second to the third level, but especially when we move on to the fourth level.

One of the great errors of our time is the confusing of the third with the fourth level or in thinking that the fourth level or the Life of Fullness is the same as or a simple continuation or extension of the third level. This is no more true of the fourth level than it is of the second and third: each involves a discontinuity and a transcending of the previous level. Many accomplished artists and intellectuals commit this fallacy of confusing the creating the harmonizing/aesthetic level with the Life of Fullness. But no amount of success and satisfaction at the third level will quantitatively result in arriving at the fourth level.

Like the second and third levels of this nested hierarchy, the Life of Fullness requires the satisfaction of the needs of each previous level and then a complete break with the *exclusive* reliance on the values and working processes of that level. This break or discontinuity is arrived at by discovering the limits of those values and working processes for anything beyond that level. So, in order to continue the Questing that is both our propensity and our destiny, we require the discontinuity that opens us up to go beyond or transcend each level to the next.

This is clearer to see in a more familiar development in our history, namely in our society's transition from second level achieving to that of the third level. The height of the second level, creating the useful, is probably the achievement of the automated assembly line, and an effective distribution system, that is, an efficient economy. No matter how well this is done, it does not result in satisfying the creating the harmonizing/aesthetic level, which would require the economy to be not only efficient but also equitable and just, based on an emerging awareness of our Oneness in a nascent form. On the former level, the primary, requisite criterion is that of usefulness. On the creating the harmonizing/aesthetic level, usefulness ceases to be a necessary criterion even though it *may* be an incidental quality. On this level, uniqueness, individuality, and the transutilitarian values of love and justice are the criteria. This is a qualitative, not quantitative, leap, best characterized as transcending.

In human development, as mentioned earlier, the objects of this nested hierarchical process called the Questing are less concrete and more abstract as we move up the hierarchical levels. As one reaches the third or creating the harmonizing/ aesthetic level, the object of the Questing, although expressed variously and directly in rather concrete matter—print, paint, movement, sound, or space—is really a more abstract and quite ineffable experience in the world. As one attains the fourth or Life of Fullness level, the Questing is no longer objective—that is, there is no object in our world or reality that can be sought to express it—and we are dealing with a totally abstract or transcendent realm for which we have no categories or vocabulary in our experience.

Although the Questing is driven by elemental needs and some of their culture-specific ways of expression (that is, conditioned desires and mores) at the subsistence survival level, conditioned desires not directly based on the elemental needs are added as the driving force at the creating the useful level. Then, at the creating the harmonizing/aesthetic level, we can become aware of the impetus that I call the *Yearning*, but it is confused with desire. Finally, at the fourth or Life of Fullness level, desire plays no part, and the Yearning is the sole impetus.

To begin to understand the Yearning, a moment's reflection on the nature of desire is necessary. All of our desires are the result of the conditioning process through enculturation (or acculturation if we come into contact with a different culture, such as when we move to another country or region of the world), whereas our elemental needs of the first level are inborn. In other words, desires are learned, as well as the socially approved ways of satisfying them and our elemental needs. Although the desire-conditioning process is universal in human societies, the specific desires and socially approved forms of satisfying them will vary from society to society.

Also, the desire-conditioning process begins with desires based on our elemental needs, but it goes on to desires based less and less on these needs and more and more on what the society has learned works for its own and its members' survival. However, these conditioned desires will always entail concrete objects and experiences in our conditioned world. By the time we reach the third or creating the harmonizing/aesthetic level of Questing, we can become aware of the Yearning, but it is usually confused with desire. At this level, the object of the Questing is still expressed in this world of our experience, but we also find that it points beyond to something quite ineffable. This latter is the realm of the Yearning in which the Questing has no objects, let alone experiences, categories, or vocabulary to express it.

The Yearning is the central impetus of our very being and is also known as the still, small voice within. But why is it known as still and small? Since the Yearning is not survival-based and does not appear to have any survival value, society does not, through the enculturation process, recognize it, let alone encourage or provide any sanctions for it. Is it any wonder why that inner voice has come to appear still and small? This would seem to preclude any outlet for the powerful and primal energy—the *passion*—of the Yearning. However, we are conditioned to divert this passion or energy of the Yearning to a counterfeit expression, which is illusory but appears quite real to our survival-based worldview. This counterfeit is what we call *desire*, the result of the desire-conditioning process just discussed.

To understand desire more fully, we must go back to one of our earliest and incessant conditionings that is summed up in the simple message that is continually aimed at each one of us: "You are *lacking* and *inadequate* as you are." This message is at the heart of the enculturation process and is certainly true and necessary when it concerns survival: for the purpose of survival, each of us is lacking and inadequate as we come into the world. Society, with its myopic view and with the best of intentions, through its various agencies, such as family, school, religion, employment, and government, conditions this message in us so that each of us will be maximally receptive to the enculturation.

Each of society's agencies tends to see itself as essential to, and perhaps even the focal point of, the enculturation process. As a result, there is a little addendum to the basic message, which becomes: "You are lacking and inadequate as you are, but if you stick with us (that is, do things our way or follow our conditionings), we will get you from here, lacking and inadequate, to there," a socially approved and conditioned goal, sometimes less vague than at other times. The family promises growing up successfully, religion—salvation, peers—approval, schools—graduation, employers or gangs—tangible rewards and status, and so on. And these promises are what we come to value and desire, together with their associated affective rewards. In such a manner, all of the objects of the *Desiring process*, such as those we call goals, purposes, ambitions, expectations, and hopes (remember that the Hope process is foundational in the enculturation process) are conditioned in us. This is the primary way we learn to desire.

However, the Desiring process has the effect of buffering or masking the Yearning and of diverting its energy. Now you can see why the spiritual literature, both Eastern and Western, is so replete with the injunction to subdue the desires. This, of course, reflects the usual kind of misunderstanding of the underlying truth. We can no more get rid of our desires, which are most effectively conditioned in us, than we can get rid of our fears or hopes. No, the task here is the same as with the Fear and Hope processes: We must transcend the Desiring process through first recognizing its illusoriness, namely that something outside of us can achieve for us that inward Fullness which can be attained only through the Second Journey. Then, we find that there is no need for desire as we discover the principle that *each of our needs is met*. (More on that later.) This is why I call it the Life of Fullness.

The Desiring process is the energetic, more active manifestation of the Hope process. It is the means through which we activate any expression of the Hope process by sublimating the energy of our Yearning. The Desiring process is based upon an unexamined assumption that has become the credo of our enculturated First Journey, namely that the aim of life is *happiness*; of course, happiness always depends so much upon something—involving experiences, persons, or objects external to us and in the world—*happening* to us. This is an integral part of that illusory worldview that keeps failing us over and over again but in which we persist.

As with the Fear and Hope processes, we pay a dear price when the Desiring process is allowed to go unchecked in the rampant expression greatly encouraged, especially in our society, often as a very basic driving force of our economy. One particularly grievous contemporary manifestation of this is what we call addiction. This is the Desiring process gone awry. Along with the mental illness and violence that have become endemic in our society, addiction reflects the ends to which people are driven in reaction to the sense of betrayal they feel when the actual Yearning is so ignored and unexplored while our society provides only the myriad paltry counterfeits. Addiction, the exaggeration of the Desiring process, which is in turn nested in the Hope process, is the granting of one's own power to something external, whether a substance or an experience, and is the pursuit of happiness at any cost; it is a denial of the inner life.

In marked contrast to the pursuit of happiness, *Joy* does not happen to us; there is no external agent or cause. It is not a goal like happiness but rather "the echo of God's life in us." That is, Joy is what wells up from within when we discover who we truly are in the Life of Fullness. The pursuit of happiness becomes trivial when the Joy that is our birthright is revealed.

There is a more pervasive manifestation of the Desiring process that occurs when one does not become aware of the Yearning. The Yearning is still there but hidden and ignored by the enculturation, which provides no categories for its recognition since it has no survival value. However, such a powerful impetus as the Yearning still cannot be ignored, and we mistranslate or pervert its energy into a form of the Desiring process that I call "seeking distractions and diversions." Since we are not aware of this power as Yearning and have no way of channeling or expressing it, we react to it as something bothersome or troubling, something to be drained off or avoided. Unless we awaken to the Yearning, this leads to what can become a lifelong inclination to seek distractions and diversions from even the slightest awareness of our despair, namely, that the Hope process is not and cannot be fulfilling. The effect is to delay our bottoming-out and the concomitant awareness of our despair. (The importance of such awareness as part of a developmental process necessary to the Second Journey will be explored more fully in the next chapter.)

It is important to note here that nothing in and of itself is a distraction or diversion, but anything can serve as such, whether it is a single event, person, object, or an ongoing situation or relationship. This life provides a plethora: games, relationships, occupations, and travel, as well as political, religious, or social groups, and even useful objects. In other words, we can be quite ingenious in appropriating a situation or object as a distraction or diversion from any awareness of our despair, and in such manner live what may conventionally be called a "full" life, based primarily upon the quantity of distractions and diversions and later upon the "quality" of them as gauged by the values of our level (second or third) of awareness this side of the Life of Fullness.

In our time, many use their occupations or professions in this way to avoid the calling of their Yearning. Others switch or seek relationships for this purpose. Games, travel, places, and things; intellectual, religious, emotional, or physical pursuits; as well as drugs and food, will serve as well. The difficulty in all of this is that we cannot avoid the eventual habituation that leads to boredom, ennui, or addiction. Each of these requires larger doses of what got us to that point in the misbegotten belief that we can storm the gates of heaven through sheer quantity, even of what we consider pleasurable. The gates of heaven will not yield to this but only to that which transcends the merely pleasurable.

Only the Joy that comes so unexpectedly as a by-product of yielding to the Yearning transcends pleasure. It is not that we have to give up pleasure; rather, it is that in becoming aware of our Yearning, we can discover that which is beyond and qualitatively exceeds pleasure—the joy, ecstasy, and exaltation of the Life of Fullness. The Yearning is of our nature, but like sexuality, it is only expressed as the result of a confusing developmental process, as has been described. When we become aware of it at the third or creating the harmonizing/aesthetic level, it is confused with desire. Unlike desire, however, the Yearning is not and cannot be conditioned. It is fundamental to our *emergent human nature*, which is a concept worth exploring here.

Like the concept *emergent evolution*, which has more general biological, anthropological, and historical applications, emergent human nature involves the expression, at succeeding levels, of wholly new and unexpected characteristics or qualities. This process can be observed both historically and in individuals. Historically, we can see this in society's moral development, for example, in the emergence of humane treatment for the elderly, the mentally ill, and prisoners. In the individual, this can be seen in the emergence of such developments as sexuality, creating the useful abilities, the moral sense, harmonizing/aesthetic creativity, and the search for meaning or fullness at succeeding levels. There is no necessity in any of these developments; they are potentials of emergent human nature that may or may not be realized depending on the individual.

Just as our sexuality is primarily biologically or genetically based, but its expression is socially or environmentally determined or influenced, so too such developments as the moral sense, harmonizing/aesthetic sensibilities, and the search for meaning or fullness are based not on genetics or the environment but on the *Umbilicum process*, yet their expressions are socially or environmentally influenced and will vary from society to society and from time to time.

It is through the Umbilicum process that we find the Source of our Questing and the Yearning. Here let us note we are not dealing with spatiotemporal categories, so we cannot say the Umbilicum process and the Source are either inside or outside of us but rather that they are of a continuity that is both within and without. They can be seen as a nonlocal field or hierarchy of fields that access us and to which we have access—the ultimate source of our emergent human nature, which is a dynamic flux, whether considering an individual (ontogeny) or humankind as a whole (phylogeny).

This emergent human nature is revealed to us as we progress from one level to the next in the developmental process of our four nested hierarchical levels. At the first level (subsistence survival), the impetus is primarily biological, with conditioned desires emerging from and based on the biological drives to which they are consequently alloyed. At the second level (creating the useful), the impetus is primarily conditioned desires based on assuring continued successful survival. At the third level (creating the harmonizing/aesthetic), the impetus is a confused attempt at mixing these conditioned desires with the emergent Yearning process. Then at the fourth level (the Life of Fullness), the impetus is purely the Yearning. The Yearning is not a spatiotemporal process, so that in a sense it is always there (that is, omnipresent), but due to the enculturation process, it is simply unlikely for us to be aware of it before the third level.

Note that these are nested hierarchical levels of awareness, with each succeeding level subsuming the previous level or levels.

Until we become aware of the Yearning, the most we can be aware of within are the drives and conditioned desires that motivate or push us on. As we become aware of the Yearning, we come to realize that we are not being pushed or motivated by it, but rather we are being *pulled* toward the transcendent or the Life of Fullness. This pulling or level of the Questing can reveal what is pulling, yet it is something for which we have no word. The closest we can come to describing this in a word comes from the ancient Greek *Areté*, which is nearly untranslatable. (We might have used the Latin-based term *virtue*, except that it has come to have an increasingly erroneous and unfortunately moralistic connotation.)

Areté refers to the excellence or highest expression of anything. The examples usually proffered are: the *Areté* of a racehorse is to run swiftly, of a cup is to hold liquid, and so on. But what is the *Areté* of a human being, that most complex development of evolution? That is not an ordinary question for which there is an answer as though we were asking about a fact in the spatiotemporal world of our everyday experience or reality. It is rather what may be called an ultimate question relating to the realm that transcends the everyday and in which answers are not stated but lived as a consequence of continuing exploration. Thus, we see that the Areté of a human is not something that can be stated, but rather is a unique path to be discovered through exploration and unfoldment. (More will be said on this later.)

Now let us look at an important aspect of the Umbilicum process that we experience but are unable to articulate, except in such terms as *intuition*, which like the term *instinct*, is a catchall that does not really explain or help us explore the process. Remember that the Umbilicum process works at least in both the direction of sending to and receiving from the Source, and it is working at all four nested hierarchical levels, where each succeeding level subsumes the prior level. Thus, the boundaries of these levels, unlike geographic and normally logical boundaries, are quite porous and fuzzy, more like life and the organic. At each of these levels, especially when we have reached the limits of a level—that is, succeeded at that level—we will receive communications from the Source in the mode of the succeeding level. This is what we often call intuition because it is inexpressible at our present level of awareness or consciousness.

I like to call these received communications *glimpses* or *whispers* (to use metaphors of sensory perception for that which is transsensory) because they usually do not come thunderously or even like the boisterous everyday world of our senses, but more faintly and gently. The shortcoming is not with the transmitter but with the receiver. The difficulty here is with our powers of reception at whatever is our current level of awareness; since they are so inexpressible, these glimpses or whispers are often dismissed outright, instead of simply acted on, which is what needs to be done. When we do act on them, quite remarkable things occur in our lives, depending on the level of awareness we have attained. At the level of creating the useful, it is called invention or discovery, whether concrete, like the wheel, steam engine, and computer, or abstract, like mores, laws, and institutions. At the creating the harmonizing/aesthetic level, we call it creativity or artistry. And at the level of the Life of Fullness, it is called *Revelation*.

These communications from the Source all begin for us at the prior level as glimpses or whispers, starting at the subsistence survival level (perhaps with a glimpse for a tool or a constituent element of it); but once the transition is made to the succeeding level, acting on them becomes almost routine, especially for those individuals in the vanguard. So, the Source is always gesturing and calling through the Umbilicum process. As has been said by a most sagacious teacher, what we need are the "eyes to see and the ears to hear" those glimpses or whispers.

Revelation, like its precursors that we have called whispers and glimpses, requires an openness and a will to respond without regard to our dearly held goals or purposes. Just as whispers or glimpses are for acting on, so it is with Revelation. Although whispers or glimpses are usually experienced as onetime affairs, not so with Revelation, which, if there is the requisite evolving openness, will continue pouring forth as the marvelous process it is. In effect, Revelation responds to the openness in the individual with an even greater open-endedness.

The more we trust, receive, and act on a revelation, the more will pour forth from it; more accurately, the more will we be aware of the fullness of the revelation. I am describing all of this using our ordinary language, which makes it sound like Revelation takes place in and over time, but that is not the case and is illusory. So let us remember that Revelation is of the Life of Fullness and is not a spatiotemporal phenomenon, although we must respond to it *in* this world, but not *of* it. In this way, we discover our divine capacity to express the Life of Fullness in the world.

A revelation is a response of the Source according to our needs. It manifests as a challenge to our awareness, and our response to it, as characterized above, will be "muscle building," spiritually speaking. An excellent analogy here from the third level of awareness is the inspiration that comes to the composer or artist, such as Bach or Michelangelo, and that is then manifested or unfolded as their creation in the spatiotemporal realm. The same is true of intellectuals, scientists, and mathematicians, such as Pascal, Newton, Kant, Einstein, and Heisenberg. In each case, the recipient of the inspiration is unable to trace it back to anything in this world but is able to give it expression based upon an intensive and extensive preparation of mind or awareness that itself could not account for the creation. Such inspiration is the form that Revelation takes at the creating the harmonizing/aesthetic level of awareness, at which level the artist, the scientist, and the intellectual are working. In any such case, their creativity lies in their acting in the world upon the inspiration that has been given. Such action is "muscle-building" and serves to keep the inspiration flowing.

As we shall see later, there is a Practice for the Second Journey that can serve to prepare us to transcend the ordinary, so that we will be able to respond to the extraordinary—that is, Revelation—thus enabling us to act without our usual conditioned impediments. The Practice is a kind of preparatory workout enabling us to participate in the ultimate spiritual muscle-building of responding actively to Revelation so as to keep our awareness open to its flow.

To summarize, humans are endowed with a propensity called the Questing, which is a nesting hierarchical process paralleling our four hierarchical levels of awareness, beginning at the subsistence survival level. At succeeding levels, including the second or creating the useful level, the object of the Questing becomes less concrete and more abstract and ineffable, until a dawning awareness of the unconditioned Yearning emerges at the third level. At this level, the Yearning is confused with conditioned desires. Here one must reach the limits of the creating the harmonizing/aesthetic level so as to be able then to transcend to the fourth level of pure Yearning in the Life of Fullness.

When the Yearning is ignored, we pervert its energy to the Desiring process, the way in which we find expression for the Hope process. Seeking distractions and diversions is a widely encouraged form of this. A dangerous exaggeration of the Desiring process that results from ignoring the Yearning and from the consequent sense of betrayal is called addiction. The Yearning in us is our calling to and from the Source. The Source is always calling to us in the forms appropriate to our level of awareness. (In the spiritual literature, this is called the Grace of God, about which more will be said later.)

When we act on this calling or communication from the Source, it is called invention or discovery at the second level, as well as in the transition to that level; it is called creativity or artistry at the third level, as well as in the transition thereto; it is called Revelation at the fourth level, as well as in the transition to that level.

The Questing and the Yearning are manifestations of the Umbilicum process, which can be seen as our two-way, nonmaterial connection to—or better yet, our continuum with—the Source. At the Yearning level of the Questing, we can become aware of a pulling toward the Life of Fullness. This is best described by the ancient Greek term *Areté*, which refers to our excellence or highest expression that can only be discovered by acting on the Yearning and the callings from the Source in the forms of glimpses, whispers, or Revelation. What are simply occasional glimpses or whispers at a particular level become practically routine revelations at the succeeding level, when they are acted on so as to reveal their fullness. This is our emergent human nature that reveals our *Areté*.

5

DESPAIR AND THE HUMAN TRAGEDY

The title of this chapter may not be so inviting, but an understanding of these concepts, their genesis, how they manifest in our lives, what they entail, and how we must relate to our experience of them is essential to making any effort toward the Second Journey, leading to the Life of Fullness.

As mentioned earlier, societies are much like dinosaurs: they have tremendous bulk and can crush you if you interfere with their collective goals and purposes; they are basically concerned with survival, primarily their own and secondarily the individual's. No society has evolved, so far, to the point of encouraging anything beyond the third level of awareness, which I include as part of our Life of Survival on the First Journey.

Society does not encourage the Second Journey into the fourth level of awareness or consciousness because that does not appear to have survival value, society's fundamental criterion. The *apparent* exception to this is society's encouragement of religion, but upon closer scrutiny, we see that society's interest in and support of religion have always been primarily on the basis of its utility as an instrument of social control, stability, and cohesion, all of which are necessary to a society's survival. Society is not stupid where survival is concerned; rulers, chiefs, kings, and those in control learned long ago that a priest is much more cost-effective than tens or even hundreds of policemen when it comes to social control.

There is still much confusion between religion and the spiritual. In addition to earlier comments on the meaning of the Latin root *religio* and how religion manifests and works, we need to be aware that religion is an early stage in our evolution to an awareness of the spiritual. In the past, our framework and view of the cosmos were simply a projection outward of our very earthly political situation and social structure, reflecting our experiences therein.

In the time of powerful chiefs, rulers, and kings, when subjects were viewed as the equivalent of the leader's children, the cosmos was seen as ruled by an all-powerful and distant Father-god. This view virtually mirrored our experience in the world, with a god (an evolutionary step toward unity from the older polytheism) at the top as supreme ruler over an anthropocentric world, and with other living (and nonliving) entities having relatively insignificant status. In the governance of the cosmos, as with earthly rulers, God had numerous functionaries to assist him (and these religions were sexist, patriarchal organizations, reflecting the society). Also included were intermediaries who could be appealed to for intercession, just as in our worldly situation. This set the pattern and became the framework of our contemporary religions (at least in the West; the East has its own appropriate variations) during the Religious era.

Further, our worldly situation was replete with magical explanations for all sorts of natural phenomena; we had a magical view of the world, and this was reflected in our religions, with which we are still living, even though we have grown, albeit unevenly, far beyond that magical view, thanks to our scientific and intellectual developments. So, we find ourselves living with fossils of the Religious Era that can no longer relate to our evolving nature, that cannot address our emergent human condition of the Yearning and the Questing for the Life of Fullness in the Post-religious Era.

Thus, the terms *religious* and *spiritual* should never be used synonymously any more than *kindergarten* and *university* should. Religion has been most important, at quite a price at times, in our moral evolution and awareness, even though it tends to the dogmatic and to closure. All of this was necessary for humanity to evolve through its youthful phase. However, religion and its modern surrogates must be transcended for those who care to begin the spiritual work of the Second Journey, which requires an openness to which the goals, purposes, and closed systems of religion, no matter how well meaning, are antithetical.

Although I am here urging an evolutionary transcendence that is of our emergent human nature, I would never deny it to anyone who feels the need for the addictive certitude, finality, and *comforts* of religion or of any of the numerous alternative closed systems currently available. By the way, the word *comfort* is a good example of a word that has fallen into misuse: contrast its current usage and meaning to its roots and original meaning of "with strength" or "to strengthen." As we shall see, only the spiritual, not religion, can truly comfort, in the best sense of the word.

Now let us look at how society's spiritual ignorance affects the individual whose Questing has evolved through the third level and who needs to make the transition to the fourth level. Remember that at the third level, the Yearning can emerge to our awareness but is confused with our conditioned desires. We can become aware of the Yearning as an ineffable mode of being, together with the glimpses or whispers that filter through; however, we tend to relate and identify all of this with the known of our world—that is, with our conditioned desires and the categories and vocabulary of our ordinary, enculturated worldview. And these are totally ineffectual for making the transition to pure Yearning.

Since society provides no sanctions or institutions to help make this transition to pure Yearning, the individual at this point seems to have no way out and comes to feel an inexpressible desolation. This is often triggered by what is called a bottoming-out experience, which occurs when a highly valued goal or purpose of ours is or appears totally frustrated. The bottoming-out experience can take any number of forms, depending on what goals or purposes are most prized. It can result from the loss of a job, not receiving an expected promotion, the loss of a loved one through death, separation, divorce, or similar disappointments. Usually, a bottoming-out leads to what I referred to earlier as a redoubling of effort, temporarily dropping out, or the taking of what appears to be a different direction—such as shifting from one area of endeavor in the world to another or changing relationships or habitat—but one that basically stays on the enculturated track.

On a much deeper and more ineffable level, there is a very different kind of bottoming-out that is triggered by the vague uneasiness, at first, and then the deepening desolation one experiences upon becoming aware that achieving many of this life's goals and purposes does nothing to fulfill one's Yearning. Unlike the previously described ordinary form of it, this deeper kind of bottoming-out experience results not just from the disappointment of particular hopes and desires; it results from a developing awareness of the bankruptcy of our hopes and of hoping in general—that is, from an awareness of our despair (which we will explore more fully shortly).

Many who find themselves at this stage are tempted by and succumb to what appears to be a way out, of which there are a plethora of advocates. I refer here to the numerous seminars, groups, and cults that have surfaced to supplant the retreating majority of organized religions and that beckon to the spiritually starved today. Many of these are well meaning and led by very sincere individuals who *seem* to be helping people embark on the Second Journey. But these latter-day surrogates for religions suffer from the same inherent error that has doomed organized religions to an evolutionary dead end. In order to understand the shortcomings of these many efforts, we must become aware of an important characteristic of the Second Journey that can become evident from even the most cursory examination of the lives of mystics.

First, I must correct some gross misunderstandings regarding the mystic, as well as a current confusion regarding this term. The mystic is that person who, having reached the limits of the third level of awareness, has the courage to enter the No-man's-land of the transition to the Life of Fullness of the fourth level. To me, the mystic is the most practical of persons, who is concerned not just with the short-term, bottom-line survival needs of life, but also with the compelling and ultimately practical questions and needs of becoming fully human.

Further, to clear up that regrettable and sloppy confusion found in so much of contemporary usage, the term *mystic* and the mystic have nothing to do with magic. Magic is our term for explaining phenomena of which we do not understand the underlying principles. For example, much of what is explained today by the principles of modern chemistry had at some time past been considered magic and may still be by the ignorant or gullible. Magic is in the eye, or lack thereof, of the beholder. Ask any magician.

Now back to the mystic and the Second Journey and that most important characteristic of both. A mystic may have started out as part of a group, but he or she made that Second Journey alone! And that is the only way it can be done, not that a guide who has made the journey cannot be of great help in finding one's own unique path. But do note that this journey is not made in a group, but solo, as in learning to fly, an apt analogy here. As with flying, the ideas and concepts (the bridges, so to speak) can be introduced in a group, but the actual activity must be learned solo, with the guidance of one who has been there. Even this guidance aims at the individual's being able to make the Second Journey alone.

It would be at least amusing, if it were not so pathetic, that people who would not consider going to a physician, dentist, or accountant in a group blithely assume that the Second Journey is to be done in a group. That, of course, is a conditioning acquired through organized religion, which has learned well the principles of group psychology for the purposes of social control, stability, and cohesion, none of which were ever in the minds of their putative founders. Remember, I am not antireligion any more than I am antikindergarten, antiyouth, or antischool. Religion is a necessary and desirable stage in our development. Much can be learned that can be of use up into the third level of awareness, but religion is incompetent beyond that level—except perhaps unintentionally, as when it preserves the sayings or writings of the mystics that can serve as an assurance and even an inspiration for those at the limits of the third level.

Although there are rare, exceptional individuals to be found in them, these religions certainly do not advocate the essence of what these mystics have done: leaving the flock to go it alone on the Second Journey. Remember that the priests, ministers, rabbis, mullahs, bishops, popes, roshis, or other functionaries are only very rarely of the caliber of the reputed founders and mystics of their respective traditions. One could say that organized religions as we have known them are really for the childhood and, at most, the adolescence of our species, and for that they have been invaluable in preserving and transmitting many higher values for the human community, even though accompanied by the unnecessary baggage of dead ritual, outgrown practices, and retarding symbols.

Now that we see where the error of group practice in spiritual matters comes from, we can also see why so many of these well-meaning seminars, groups, and cults persist in this practice. But even well-meaning sincerity is really no excuse for error or mis-understanding. There is no question that the bridging ideas and concepts or framework of the Second Journey can be introduced in a group. But once they are grasped, then it is time for their practice or application in our lives, and this practice will be expressed uniquely by each individual who embarks. In other words, *there is no "The Path"* on which we follow a leader or savior to the promised land. However, *there is a unique path, not a group path, for each one who makes the Second Journey* into the Life of Fullness. And this is why all of these groups will remain ineffectual at doing anything more than just introducing some bridging ideas and concepts of the transition from the third level, which, even if they are the words of a sincere leader, are usually derivative from other writings or, at most, the attempted articula-tions of some glimpses or whispers the leader has had. This latter action is an error, too. Remember, glimpses and whispers are not for articulating, but for acting upon. And that is a distinction that this society—especially some of our institutions, such as religion, politics, and academia—has difficulty in making. We too often think that *saying* or *thinking* something is the equiva-lent of *doing* it.

What, then, is the attraction of these groups, seminars, and cults? Since they are ineffectual, they must provide some deep satisfaction for their adherents. Here we must probe deeply for what moves human beings, and we find ourselves in the Umbil-icum process through which we become aware of the Yearning at the third level of awareness. This does not mean that the Yearn-ing, as well as our *Areté*, is not present at all levels. The Yearning is as fundamental to humans as their biological drives, although the latter and their conditioned derivatives need to be satisfied before we can become aware of the Yearning.

The concept of *Yearning to be One* is one of the most helpful expressions of the Yearning in attempting to understand it and the Oneness to which it points. At the fourth level of awareness, this manifests as the Yearning to be One with the Cosmos or God or the Ultimate. At the third level, this manifests as the Yearning to be One with Beauty or Harmony or any of the numerous expressions thereof. At the second level, this manifests as the Yearning to be One with our inventions and discoveries, whether these be devices, formulas, places, principles, institutions, or expressions thereof. At the first level, the Yearning manifests as the Yearning to be One with the food, water, sexual, maternal, and shelter/protection sources in our lives. This latter Yearning to be One can be seen most clearly in many tribal practices still extant or preserved and oftentimes symbolically transformed but quite recognizable in religious practices, such as the sacrament of communion for Christians and the ceremony of the Passover Seder for Jews.

We are meant to transcend all of these lower manifestations of the Yearning to be One as we evolve through our first three levels of awareness. Until we attain the fourth or Life of Fullness level and truly become aware of our Oneness, we will exhibit the lower manifestations in various mixes depending upon individual evolution. So, even if one is near the limits of the third level, the individual may still exhibit lower manifestations of this Yearning to be One, especially that manifestation colloquially referred to as the *lifeboat experience*, with which we may be quite familiar, even if we have not articulated it.

The most dramatic form of the lifeboat experience arises in some extreme situation in the company of others in which there is at least the appearance of our survival being threatened imminently, yet we are able to survive it. (Such a threat need not be physical.) The lifeboat experience has been the stuff of cults and religious conversions for centuries, and in our times, many have experienced it in group therapy and other group motivational situations. The Yearning to be One manifests here in an otherwise inexplicable bond among the survivors or participants, which keeps them coming together afterwards, even if they share few or no other interests. The affective dimension of this experience can be quite intense, expressed as a strong identification with the group involved and, derivatively, its members. This manifestation of the Yearning to be One is the main basis for the attraction of these groups, cults, and seminars described earlier. We will now turn to why individuals coming to these groups feel that their very survival is imminently threatened.

In any society, successful survival requires that the individual has been enculturated into at least the second or creating the useful level of awareness. This is usually called being a productive member of society. There are many who reach the limits of this level and transcend to the third level where they can express themselves in what we call in our society the arts, science, theology, philosophy, and such. At this level, societies that have gone beyond enculturating for the subsistence survival level to the creating the useful level of awareness for most of their members are then in a position to make the transition to providing sanctions and institutions for the encouragement and expression of third-level awareness. At first, in our society, for example, this is usually in some form of schooling and then in other institutions, such as academia, the theater, institutes, academies, as well as in the many religious, educational, research, and publishing organizations. (So many of the inter- and intranational conflicts today are between societies that *have* versus those that *have not* made that transition.)

Of those persons who are thus encouraged and who reach well into the third level of awareness, some will discover the limits because their Questing no longer finds satisfaction; this is because at this level none of the objects or experiences can truly address the Yearning, that new form of the Questing of which these persons are becoming aware.

At this point, most react quite predictably, as they would to any ongoing frustration. When people keep bumping up against limits, they tend either to give up or to redouble their efforts or to take what appears to be another direction. These latter two reactions only delay, often quite distractingly (for example, aiming for twice as much money or a new mate, job, or career), the inevitable and necessary giving up. But think about what the alternative of giving up implies. It means the giving up of hope, and remember how deeply conditioned the Hope process is and how alloyed with the Fear process it is. That is why I call this stage of awareness *Despair*, based on its Latin roots meaning "without hope." We do not readily consent to such radical giving up of hope, which is Despair. Remember that we have become hope addicts, and the withdrawal inherent in this new awareness of Despair can, if we are not ready for the Second Journey, elicit in us the most awesome expression of the Fear process: there does not appear to be a palpable object, but only an intense anxiety or *Angst*.

The awareness of our Despair, this awareness that there are no hopes, no hoping, is also experienced as the *Nothingness*. When our lives have heretofore been filled by the Hope process, this awareness of its illusoriness will be interpreted by our ordinary mind and feelings as Emptiness or Nothingness rather than simply as our natural state. To our ordinary consciousness, that upon which we have relied so much is no longer to be relied upon, is no longer there—thus, the Emptiness or Nothingness. (For a very interesting treatment of this theme, see Michael Novak's *The Experience of Nothingness*.) Remember, the contents of the Hope process are always in the future, and this awareness of our Despair is also interpreted as the absence of a future. Our ordinary consciousness is not capable of living without a future and without its creation, time—that is, not capable of simply living in the now.

There is another general reaction to the awareness of our Despair that must be averted because it leads only backwards and is self-indulgent at a low level. This quite normal reaction is an emotional one, reflecting nothing more than the dark side of our affective conditioning, and perhaps some projections of the light side. That is, in reaction to the awareness of our Despair and as a last-ditch effort to avoid the necessary transcending to the unknown next level of awareness, we will tend to project Hell and Heaven from the contents of our distorted affective and mental conditionings. (This reaction may help to explain the prevalence of such *Sturm und Drang* in so much religious writing, as well as in a lot of the good Existentialist writing.)

What I have been describing are the outlines of the necessary steps that we follow, together with some of the expected reactions we may have, in discovering the limits of the third level of awareness. This is a relatively new stage in the evolution of humankind; as far as we know, probably only a few thousand years old, dating to some time after the dawn of civilization. It is civilization that provides the conditions that lead to the leisure necessary for some individuals to attain the third level of awareness. When some of these individuals discover the limits of this level of awareness, they are faced with a most terrible realization. Up to this point, the alloying of the Hope and Fear processes, starting out as necessary to successful survival, have become so deeply conditioned that we come to believe that they are of our human nature rather than just of the human norm.

This is when we can discover that Despair, being without the illusions of hope, is really our human nature, and that the Hope process is necessary only to mitigate the ravages of that other illusion, the Fear process. Here we have also become aware of the Yearning and that there are no objects or experiences in our conditioned world that can address the Yearning. In other words, at this transition stage, there is nothing for which we can hope. But this doing without hope exposes us to that form of fear without an object that we call Angst. And this feels as though our very existence is imminently threatened, which sets us up for the *lifeboat experience*.

It is during this stage that we are most vulnerable and attracted to the entreaties of the groups, cults, and seminars that are society's modern substitutes for the failed religions and the *religio* functions they used to serve. We are desperately seeking a way to avoid giving up hope, and these groups, often most sincerely, proffer great hope. These groups are society's latest attempts to deal with this stage by providing hope and lifeboat experiences, which result in bonding and much good feeling but, as with religions, no transcendence to the next level of awareness.

The alternative to these counterfeits entails becoming radically aware of the limits of our enculturation, which can serve us well for survival purposes but which consists of so many impediments to the transition to the fourth level of awareness. But having arrived at this stage, we do not easily give up our exclusive reliance on the very conditionings that led to our successful survival. There is a wonderfully appropriate Zen story about two monks who reached a very large lake during a journey. They determined that the best solution would be to build a raft to cross it. They did so and crossed the lake. On the other side, one of the monks insisted on carrying the raft along. Soon he was complaining about the burden. The other monk responded, in effect, that the raft had served its purpose and was no longer needed, and so they should be rid of it. We are much like that in wanting to persist in those conditionings that led to our successful survival, even though they can be impediments to the Second Journey.

In fact, it is these successful survival conditionings that are seen by us and others in our society as our strengths. These strengths are continually being reinforced in our experiences. When we discover the limits of the third level—that is, when our strengths are of no use in transcending to the fourth level—we become aware of our Despair and the attendant Angst. As long as we cherish these strengths so much and do not simply limit them to our Life of Survival, we are doomed to only our awareness of the Despair and our Angst. This is what I have called the Human Tragedy, in the ancient Greek sense of the term tragedy, as mentioned before, in which the protagonist is brought to a downfall as the result of pride or hubris in what were considered strengths or heroic qualities. How insightful! This is the height of the human condition when it is limited to the Life of Survival; that is the *Human Tragedy*!

Here it would be well to clarify a most pervasive confusion that exists today in our society, and that is the confusion of the terms and states called *Despair* and *depression*, and the lack of a clear distinction between them. We have come far enough in the elucidation of our new framework that we can make such a distinction. Depression is the result of the disappointment of a specific hope—that is, a purpose or a goal. We have all experienced this in the hopes associated with relationships, jobs, careers, acquisitions, and outcomes. Depression can arise from, for example, being dropped in a relationship, not receiving an anticipated promotion or raise, no new car or dress that was wanted, or no sale or contract after an extended pitch or negotiation. But that very depression can easily be lifted subsequently by the satisfaction of the hope that was originally disappointed or by the fulfillment of a similar or greater hope.

In the case of Despair, we have something that is qualitatively quite different. Despair, unlike depression, is not the disappointment of a hope or hopes; it is the realization that the previously hoped-for objects and experiences are not capable of leading to the fullness now required by our emerging awareness of the Yearning at the third level. And that leads to seeing that hopes and hoping are illusory. This is Despair and cannot be lifted or erased by the satisfaction of any hope. It develops due to the incommensurateness of our encultured Hope process, even when satisfied, and the awareness of our Yearning. Thus, Despair is the consequence of our Yearning being ignored and unfulfilled while we still rely upon the illusory Hope process.

It is this confusing of depression and Despair that dogs the psychiatric, psychological, and other helping professions today. Psychotherapy of various kinds can be quite effective in treating depression—that is, in coping with the disappointments of hopes—but it is totally incompetent in dealing with Despair. The reasons for this are quite simple. Modern psychology, on which psychotherapy is based, is in turn based mainly on the study of *human norms* and deviations therefrom, rather than on the exploration of *human nature*. The purpose of psychotherapy, protestations to the contrary notwithstanding, is to restore the individual as a productive member of society or to socially approved relationships; in other words, to reinforce the enculturation. This is a worthy and needed objective when dealing with the misenculturated. Psychotherapy has been found to be of limited value in dealing with the malenculturated, however, where behavior modification would most likely be the most effective treatment. (Boot camp–type sentencing and prisons indicate a currently surfacing awareness of this.)

Admittedly, some great psychologists, such as William James, Carl Jung, and Abraham Maslow, have gone beyond psychology to explore spiritual human nature; but in doing this, they were no longer functioning as conventional psychologists but rather more in keeping with the root meaning of the term *psyche* (soul, self, mind). But the great majority of those practicing psychotherapy are not aware of this vital distinction; the result is that many who are in Despair and who turn to psychotherapy are inappropriately treated as depressed, ignoring the psyche or Soul, and this is a great disservice.

Further, calling Despair "clinical depression" is not accurate and does not help. The deeper depressions that are experienced by so many and that we are so aware of today simply reflect the addictiveness of the Fear and Hope processes and the severity of the withdrawal experienced by those who are lacking in the successful survival skills required to achieve the conditioned goals or purposes that are the objects of their Hope process. For these people, psychotherapy can be effective in helping them on the way to successful survival.

Despair, on the other hand, requires not a psychotherapist but a guide (more on the guide later). Again, lest I be misunderstood, I am not antipsychology or antipsychotherapy. Psychology, especially the fields of perception, learning, and human development, is invaluable to this entire present undertaking, but it is inappropriate for attempting to understand the Second Journey and the Life of Fullness. Also, psychotherapy—and its stronger form or expression, behavior modification—is, as I have said, essential for correcting the extensive and increasing misenculturation and malenculturation that we see today and that serve to preclude successful survival for so many. But the fields of psychology and psychotherapy have these inherent limits that need to be acknowledged, especially in the confusing of Despair with depression.

As we shall see, what needs to be done with our Despair is to *embrace* it as the friend it is for having brought us to this opportune point in our life. Persisting in our exclusive reliance upon the Life of Survival conditionings without becoming aware of and then embracing our Despair leads inexorably to the Tragic Life. This is that life failure which insists on using our First Journey strengths that are not only ineffectual but may also be impediments to making the transition to the fourth level of awareness on the Second Journey.

6

EMBRACING DESPAIR TOWARD THE LIFE OF FULLNESS

$\mathcal{A}$s we have seen, we had to learn the Hope process along with the Fear process in order for us to become successful survivors. Although not of our human nature, they become deeply ingrained affective conditionings of the enculturation process and consequently also become the norms of our social and psychological condition. Thus, as the dark side of our affective conditioning, the Fear and Hope processes are the main carriers of our emotional energies, which accounts for the many mental ills and phobias pervading all levels of our society. Any tampering with the Fear and Hope processes can result in some very disabling effects. This certainly occurs when, as discussed in the last chapter, we become aware of our Despair but attempt to salvage some hope which brings into play that manifestation of the Fear process we call Angst. This, in turn, may cause us to grasp at any hope that is proffered, especially if it claims to be addressing our condition, as the many groups, cults, and seminars of our time claim to do.

There is another kind of reaction that many have when they become aware of their Despair. It involves a kind of step backwards. In an effort to recapture that seemingly more innocent and simple hope of their childhood, people may embrace the very religion that failed them, or a variant thereof. They will do this in spite of their own mental or intellectual reservations or objections in a desperate attempt to recover the comfort and safety experienced at an earlier stage of their lives. Of course, one can never recapture that, although one may undergo the lifeboat experience. What is rarely understood is that the Life of Fullness is attained not by denying the intellect, which is necessary to reach the threshold, but by transcending the intellect. I never cease to be amazed at the kinds of illusions people will maintain in order to avoid growth, a change that is usually perceived as painful and thus is avoided. Further, growth in the Second Journey is not accomplished in groups, but by the individual alone, although aided by a guide in the early stages.

The first stage of this Second Journey concerns how we respond to the Despair that occurs when we discover the limits of the third level of awareness. Instead of succumbing to the entreaties of the Hope and Fear processes, which is the usual reaction, we must learn just to *be* with our Despair. For those who have acquired the taste for truthful paradox, let me quote Michael Novak from his fine book, *The Experience of Nothingness*: "Our hope is an acceptance of despair." In other words, the only hope is to be without hope. To put it succinctly and clearly, we must simply be choicelessly aware of our Despair, without judgment, so that we can see clearly what it is. Choiceless awareness, as we shall see, is perceiving without judgment and without the grid of our usual conditioned goals and purposes, and this requires practice (which we will explore in depth later). Reacting with hope and fear precludes choiceless awareness.

When we learn to be choicelessly aware of our Despair, we can discover the limitations and the illusoriness of the Hope process, that it is the necessary alloy of the Fear process. We can also discover that this alloyed process required us, for survival purposes, to delegate our own power to that which appears to be outside of us and not of the now. This delegation of our power is not necessary for, and is inconsistent with, the Second Journey, as we will see. In fact, a central aspect of this journey is to discover our *Power*, our true human nature.

Now we need to make a critical distinction between *Power* and *control*, as we will use these terms. Our enculturation for successful survival requires that we learn and exercise control over our environment, including whatever we consider to be ourselves, as well as others. The greater that control, the more we are considered successful, whether accomplished through wealth, position, status, or sheer cleverness in pandering to the wants or desires of others. Control is defined and accomplished by the manipulation of our world in accordance with the objects of our Hope and Fear processes and their derivative goals and purposes in our lives.

Although such control is useful and necessary for successful survival, it must be transcended for the Second Journey wherein we can discover our true Power. I do not use the term *Power* as synonymous with control. Power does not involve control—that is, the manipulation of our world for our goals and purposes based upon the Fear and Hope processes. Control is learned and exercised in the world; Power is discovered and explored in the Life of Fullness, where we can then see it manifested in the world. All we can do here is to point briefly at this Power so as to see that it is distinct from our everyday experience of control.

Power is of our human nature, so when we illusorily delegate it in the Fear and Hope processes, we are denying our very nature. We can get away with this while we are learning to survive and as long as we can be satisfied with simply surviving, but we must transcend control in order to embark on the Second Journey. All too often, under the guise of so-called spiritual development, people are misguidedly urged to find their way there through control, especially in dealing with the manifestations of Despair. Trying to control our Despair through the manipulation of our goals and purposes derived from the Hope and Fear processes will always fail, although we will feel better exercising control at first just because this has always made us feel better in the past.

In order to transcend the third or creating the harmonizing/ aesthetic level of awareness upon discovering its limits, we must become choicelessly aware of and then learn to embrace Despair. We can become choicelessly aware of our Despair simply by acknowledging what has become obvious but which we are conditioned not ever to admit: that there is no hope. That is, at the limits of the third level (and beyond), there are no objects or objectives in our world that can address the Yearning that has emerged to our awareness. The Hope process has been necessary for survival, but it now functions at best as a counterfeit for the Yearning and at worst, along with the Fear process, as the root of what we call mental illness. We can see now how the attainment or realization of our hopes has invariably left us briefly satisfied and then strangely disappointed in the long run as we attempt to continue the Hope process by restructuring our derivative goals and purposes.

Also, we can see how often in our lives greater satisfaction and fulfillment have occurred, not when the goal or purpose we sought was attained, but when an entirely unexpected outcome has occurred. We sometimes refer to these as flukes, but on a more sophisticated level we use the term serendipity. We may even eventually admit that most of the good things in our lives occurred that way. Such an awareness is a hint or a glimpse of the Life of Fullness in which we would discover that our vaunted control pales in the face of the Power available to us. Instead of acting on this glimpse and on others that we have and then embarking on the Second Journey, we cling to the Hope process as if our very lives depended on it. And if we are going to limit ourselves to the First Journey of successful survival, then our lives will be based on the Hope process, as well as its alloy, the Fear process, which elicit one another throughout our lives.

But if we are to begin our Second Journey based on the choiceless awareness of our Despair, then we must learn to embrace it. That is, we must not only recognize the failure of the Hope process in anything beyond survival, we must freely give it up on this journey, which we will discover entails also giving up its alloy, the Fear process, since they have become inextricably bound to one another.

Embracing our Despair is a simple, but not easy, thing to do. Doing so entails making a *turn*: a turn *away* from the ever-so-familiar world of our enculturation and conditionings and a turn *toward* the unknown. As mentioned in the first chapter, I call the familiar world of our enculturation Man's-land, and this transition phase on the Second Journey is called No-man's-land. It is No-man's-land because it is, of course, uncharted: it is not of our world of survival where we have a vocabulary and a framework to delineate it, as well as to make it seem familiar. No-man's-land is unfamiliar to us, and we must create a vocabulary and framework as we explore it. Some analogies may be helpful here. This is much more like the explorers of the Western Age of Exploration, especially when we compare this to the current and ever-so-safe equivalents of guided package tours being offered by the groups, cults, and seminars in our times. The Second Journey is actually much more like going on safari. You will need a guide, not to take the journey for you or to lecture you about it, but rather to help prepare and enable you to make the journey yourself.

No-man's-land can be seen as a boundary, a threshold, and a transition. It is the boundary of Man's-land or of our enculturated framework beyond which we must go. It is the threshold of the Second Journey on which we can discover our own unique path and transform the Questing to our *Areté*. It is the transition to the Life of Fullness in which we can discover and explore our true Power and human nature, as well as their source. And all of this is begun by the simple act of embracing our Despair as the friend that it is rather than as the enemy we have learned to perceive it to be. Despair, like pain, is our friend; they both function as early warning systems of impending disasters and as signals for us to change course.

It is thus that we begin our Second Journey toward higher consciousness, or *metanoia*, as the ancient Greeks called it. This is an awareness not based on our ordinary or everyday consciousness or worldview. We must go beyond or transcend that consciousness to enter the realm called the Life of Fullness. The two realms or consciousnesses that correlate to the First and Second Journeys have been referred to in a variety of spiritual literature as *the Lower self* and *the Higher self*. These terms, however, tend to make us think of these two concepts as entities and, consequently, as things that can be manipulated. I would like to introduce a far more accurate and dynamic way of looking at this by using the terms *Lower self-order of functioning* and *Higher self-order of functioning*.

The Lower self-order of functioning includes everything we do and learn on the First Journey: our reactions and responses, from our inborn drives to our enculturated conditionings through the first three levels of awareness. Further, whenever we say "I" or use any of our identities, we are referring to the Lower self-order of functioning. In this Lower self-order of functioning, we manipulate ourselves and our world to achieve our goals and purposes. This is the only reality for the great majority of people.

In the transition from the third level of awareness, we make ourselves available to the Higher self-order of functioning. We do not leave the Lower self-order of functioning behind; we still need to survive, and successfully. So, we still need all of the Lower self-order of functioning conditionings and abilities that do not limit us or lead to values that limit us to these lower levels of awareness.

Note that I said that transcending the third level of awareness means we make ourselves *available* to the Higher self-order of functioning. In other words, we can participate in it but not manipulate it, as we are accustomed to doing in the Lower self-order of functioning, which can only lead at most to control. So, we make ourselves available to the Higher self-order of functioning as the next stage in our Questing by giving up our exclusive reliance upon the Lower self-order of functioning, even though we continue to rely on it for our successful survival. This is possible only when we give up resisting and become aware of our Despair and go on to embrace it. Only then are we free enough of the Hope and Fear processes to surrender or make ourselves available to the Higher self-order of functioning and thus discover our true Power, which is the Life of Fullness.

7

TRANSCENDING: DISCOVERING THE SOUL

I have used the term *transcend* often, and now it would be well to look at it more closely. Obviously, it means to go beyond where you are at present. But there has been a tendency to think of this process spatially in that one moves from one space to another higher one, and this, of course, is misleading. Although it does mean exceeding or surpassing ordinary limits, a fuller grasp of it requires an understanding of what we earlier referred to as the "nested hierarchy"; that is, succeeding stages or levels in which each later stage subsumes the prior stage or stages whose limits have been surpassed. A simple analogy would be that of going to university in which one does not forget or ignore all that was learned in levels of school previously, but, building on it, one surpasses the limits of the prior learning and of the values based on those limits. So, in transcending, we do not leave anything behind except the limits we have discovered in the previous stage; thus, the succeeding stage is based on, or nested in, the previous stage, but implicit here is that one has fulfilled the prior stage successfully in its own terms and has gone on to surpass it qualitatively.

Transcending is what we do when we go from one level of awareness to the next. We do not leave the skills or abilities of the previous level behind—only the limits and the values based thereupon. All too often in the popular imagination, transcending to the spiritual means leaving the body and/or the mind behind. This is the sort of misconception that needs to be overcome here. Both the body and the mind are necessary for, and participate in, the Life of Fullness; however, their limits and associated values have to be discovered and surpassed. The body and the mind are not to be denied but transcended.

A rather ancient way of talking about transcendence involves the concept of the Soul. Unfortunately, the use of this term has degenerated to the point that now it is seen as a thing that cannot be verified in the usual ways with the senses and consequently was easily jettisoned by any positivistically based mindset. Nevertheless, the concept of a Soul can still be quite useful and generative if it is understood as a process. Since both the body and the mind are now seen not as things or entities but as dynamic processes, the Soul can now be seen as a process that is nested hierarchically in the mind, which in turn is nested in the body.

The Soul is not an entity or a thing, even though the use of that term in our language system practically restricts us to that view, and even though religious traditions have attempted to secure its thing-ness by etherializing it in some form or other. *The Soul is actually a process in which we are called to participate*, and to emphasize this, I call it the *Soul process*. It is not just a disembodied entity, but a dynamic process that is continuous with all of reality, including the body and mind. It is not something we have, but rather what we can *be* through participation in that process. The Soul process has become available to us as a species through our emergent human nature, and we become aware of it as individuals in our Yearning, when we are ready, through the Umbilicum process.

Just as emergent human nature earlier in our evolution gave us Mind, we have witnessed over the last few millennia the emergence, to our awareness, of Soul. I like to view this as simply the latest mutation in the process of evolving human nature, preceded by mind and its language-acquisition ability. Unfortunately, the story of the earliest mutants of which we have any record follows the usual pattern of degenerating into legends and caricatures, upon which religions are later founded and propagated, while the truth of the original revelations becomes increasingly obscured by the growth of the religious organizations.

The inefficacy of religions for anything beyond social control and cohesion—including First Journey moral development and temporary "feel good" lifeboat experiences—has led to the recognition by many that we have entered and now live in a *Postreligious Era*. This, in turn, has left many in a kind of "Waiting for Godot" mode, hoping that some other institution will surface to take up the slack. While many have turned to political institutions in recent times—especially Marxist, but also fascist and other totalitarian religio-states—others have converted religious institutions to political and economic ends, which is nothing new. None of this can work to attain fullness or to transcend the Religious Era. This is all the product of limited or stunted imaginations.

We have too long insisted that anything we are in awe of must be much larger than we are. (Actually, the phenomenon of an individual cell, atom, or molecule, if fully appreciated, is the most awesome.) First, our gods had to be extra large, which was understandable in the childhood of our species. Then we transferred these loyalties (and hopes or expectations) to monarchies, nations, religions, and any other institutions meeting our requirement of perceived gigantism.

We have to realize that the Post-religious Era is that of the individual person, in regard to both choice and responsibility. We are past institutional salvation and glorification, having discovered their limits and ineffectualness through, among other experiences in our times, two World Wars and increasing brutishness, both domestically and internationally. We are beginning to see that we cannot organize ourselves to salvation—that no matter how inspired the form of organization appears to be, it is still dependent for expression upon each individual consciousness involved.

I am not referring just to the obvious failures, such as communism, Christianity, nationalism, and the other organizational monstrosities they beget. Let us also look at such mythic evolving structures as democracy and capitalism, both of which we may consider to be organizational successes, purportedly based upon the importance, uniqueness, and dignity of the individual. In both cases, their foundations have been betrayed, and they have degenerated into not much more than pandering to that which is most base in their constituent members, whether businessmen, employees, consumers, communicants, or citizens. This is the normal outcome of such well-intentioned efforts as democracy and capitalism when they are attempted primarily through organization, but not based on our Oneness and not grounded in *Love* (a term we will explore more fully in a later chapter). Signs of these failures are all around us: the interminable appeals to ethics and reform; the unending herculean efforts at legislating away the continuing and ubiquitous conflicts arising from our organizational efforts; and the simplistic, reactionary cries to return to some religious roots, even if secularized.

Like technology, institutions and organizations are human creations and must be made to serve the individual person, and not the other way around, which has been the spiritually debilitating trend of modern history, if not of most of our history.

In sum, organization may work for survival, as well as contributing to our evolution to this stage, even though it cannot get us to the promised illusory heaven on earth. What we need now is something more akin to *organism*, a process much "fuzzier" (as in fuzzy logic) than organization. This cannot be built up incrementally any more than an organism can be built up solely by the simple accretion of cells. The process is far more dynamic, "fuzzy," and unitive. It begins with the individual, not with the group as in successful survival. Individuals must transcend the First Journey and embark on the Second Journey to the Life of Fullness. These persons will in turn, not purposefully but each in a unique manner, be forming not an organization but creating and participating in a greater spiritual organism, which is the transcendent Divine Being that is our *Areté* and to which Jesus, among others, was pointing.

Humans are the resultant not only of adaptions, but also of mutations or discontinuities and have evolved to both self-consciousness and the emerging awareness that we are here for more than survival. Realizing that potential awareness requires the discovery of our higher consciousness, which reveals our *Areté* or the fullness of which our nature is capable. This can be done only through individual choice and responsibility. This has been the underlying message of each of those earliest mutants of our emergent human nature, once you strip away the legends and caricatures that have grown about them.

Each of us is born into the Life of Survival, mastery of which is necessary, but not sufficient, for the Life of Fullness, another expression for the Soul process. Each must then choose the Soul process, or the way in which we take true responsibility for the gift that is our life. This must be our life project in the existentialist sense. Arriving at that point in our lives where we have the ability to make such a choice is the result of a developmental process quite analogous to sexual development and equally confusing and perplexing in our everyday world. Our evolution to self-consciousness has brought us to the emergence of a nascent higher consciousness, which must supplant our earlier gods and institutions for our loyalty and awe (most deservedly, we shall see). This higher consciousness is of a continuum with what we would call the Divine or the underlying principle of the Cosmos.

Not through any other person or any institution but only individually through the Inward Way can we discover and explore our higher consciousness. This is the *metanoia* mentioned earlier, for which we have evolved to be able to choose this potential. Choosing this Soul process as our life project is the way of discovering our unique path to our individual and cosmic fullness.

It is an amazing irony that the very science that was so positivistically inclined has, through the useful and generative frameworks of relativity and quantum mechanics, brought us to the position that all matter, whether entities or bodies, is process. Further, most thoughtful investigators (that is, those who have gone beyond the positivistic nineteenth-century views of science and their twentieth-century derivatives) no longer simplistically equate mind with brain (many current research policies notwithstanding). The brain, a most remarkable organ of the body, can now be seen as the vehicle or executor of the mind; the brain/mind is an interdependent dynamic that I call the *Mind process*.

What, then, is the Mind process? Evolutionarily speaking, the mind is a process qualitatively different from, but nesting hierarchically in, the body and its brain. The mind has enabled us to transcend in many ways the body and its limits. The mind not only has created the past and future, but can transcend the here and now by being conscious of itself. Self-consciousness is a remarkable leap in evolution, which, as we have seen, exhibits some amazing discontinuities—such as invention, creativity, and revelation—that our linear logic and implicit epistemology cannot explain. In the evolution of the mind, we have gone beyond the level of subsistence survival to the creating the useful level and then on to creating the harmonizing/aesthetic level of

awareness. Each of these evolutionary stages has required transcending the previous stage.

The next level of awareness to which we can evolve is the Life
of Fullness, which is my way of pointing to the Soul process, a
dynamic like the Mind process but qualitatively different. Not
participating in the Soul process once we become aware of our
Despair is truly to *Sin* (a term which has been the victim of much
mistranslation and misuse). Note that I use *Sin* not as a noun,
but as a verb or process. That process is best understood by going
back in our religious history to the word that was originally used
in the earliest reliable writings that came to be known as the New
Testament, which was written in ancient Greek. That word was
hamartia, which was derived from the ancient art and practice of
archery and which meant "to miss the mark." This in turn was
based on the Greek mythic view of humans as arrows that are
shot by God (or the Gods) at the target of our *Areté*. Human free
will and hubris allow us to interfere with this trajectory and thus
to miss the mark.

However, our derivative concept of sin has degenerated to
mean a violation or transgression of some externally imposed
code or law. We would do well to remember the origin of our term
sin in the ancient term and concept of *hamartia*. As we discussed
earlier, becoming aware of our Despair and of the Yearning are
practically simultaneous. We must then choose to embark on the
Second Journey to our *Areté*, which is how we consciously begin
the Soul process. Not to do this or to die without fulfilling this
journey is truly to Sin—that is, *hamartia*.

A fruitful way of looking at the Soul process is to see the Mind
process as a transcending mutation of the body in human evolution. Then, the Soul process is seen as a mutation at the next
level, nesting hierarchically upon but transcending the Mind
process. As far as we know, this mutation has been available for
just a few millennia, rather recently in terms of human evolution. Some of the earliest manifestations of this latest mutation

are recorded in our histories and literature as Krishna, Abraham, Gautama the Buddha, Socrates, Lao Tsu, Zarathustra, Jesus the Christ, Nanak, St. John of the Cross, Rumi, Al Ghazzali, as well as several other avatars and prophets, from Meister Eckhart to George Fox and Emerson in our own tradition. Obscuring the essence of this mutation in these exemplars are the legends that arise out of the popular imagination. These legends and the subsequent organized religions not only obscure the essence but also distort and pervert the original teachings, and are being made to serve as needed instruments of social control, cohesion, and stability. The essence of this mutation is that it points to the transcendent Soul process, or Higher self-order of functioning, which cannot be coerced or conditioned from without but can only be freely chosen from within by the individual who is ready.

Such readiness is evidenced by the individual's own sense or awareness of being a successful survivor (as was discussed earlier) as well as a willingness to *turn* from the comfortable known of our conditioned worldview to the seemingly uncomfortable unknown of our unfolding *Areté*. Of course, this requires both courage and discipline. We spoke of this earlier in the first chapter, but it would be well to remember that courage is derivative, based upon the strength and self-confidence that are by-products of successful survival. Courage is that bridge between thought and action in challenging situations; the willingness to act and the acting upon our convictions, not just the thinking or holding of them.

Discipline is a term that should be rescued from a limited understanding. It has the same root as the term *disciple*, one who is not conscripted or coerced but who follows voluntarily. Somehow, the error has grown in our thinking of discipline mostly as that which is imposed on someone from without. It is usually used when we want to put a pretty face on what we really mean: coercion. However, the Second Journey of transcending to the Soul process cannot be coerced, but it does require discipline. So let us clarify the meaning of this term to indicate an open-ended regimen that is self-imposed, that is sought and followed voluntarily.

There is a wonderful old saying that is most usually poorly understood: "Many are called, but few are chosen." The usual interpretation externalizes both the calling and the choosing. But this is a spiritual saying, not the usual descriptive statement of a familiar world. So, both the calling and the choosing are internal; that is, they are from deep within us. To be called is what I have described as becoming aware of the Yearning or of the still, small voice within. But the willingness to turn toward the unfamiliar unknown and the action of doing so are the choosing of the Soul process, and so very few actually choose this. To be called is necessary, but not sufficient. So many who are called go no further than finding refuge in some group or cult or mind-set that differs only in some externals from the comfortably familiar. So, "many are called by the Yearning, but few choose to respond" would be a more accurate statement or better understanding of that wonderful original saying.

Another misunderstood and misused saying, also attributed to Jesus in the Gospels, is "The meek shall inherit the Earth." This is quite true but not as usually understood and used, which is that the meek, those who submit to higher authority, will someday inherit or come out best. Used in this way, it can work wonders in social control for those in authority. But this is not what Jesus had in mind; in fact, his whole life testified to the very opposite of what this saying has come to mean. To grasp the fullness of what Jesus meant here, we must be aware of both the cultural and spiritual framework that he lived.

First, we must remember that for Jesus there were two realms or dimensions in which we live, the everyday and the higher or spiritual. In his time, the most encompassing or greatest realm imaginable was a kingdom, and so the higher realm was referred to as the "Kingdom of Heaven," while the everyday world was a manifold of kingdoms and pursuits that was the Earth. Jesus urged that "we seek first [in priority] the Kingdom of Heaven."

The realms of Earth were what nearly everyone was pursuing, whether in terms of wealth, control, or status; and that was the most that the meek could attain. He knew and stated quite clearly that going for the Kingdom of Heaven required great courage and audacity, not meekness. So, "The meek shall inherit the Earth" was really intended as a disparaging remark at least, and at most an ironic consolation.

Whether we refer to this transcending realm as the Kingdom of Heaven, the State of Bliss, the Tao, Nirvana, or the Life of Fullness, we are pointing at the same Soul process or Higher self-order of functioning in the individual. This is the latest mutation in human evolution and is of our emergent human nature. It is available to us if and when we are ready. That is, the choice is ours once we become aware of and embrace our Despair in the turn toward the Life of Fullness. This choice is made alone, and making it, one feels so lonely, too, because there are no sanctions or agencies in the world for doing it.

At this point, courage and audacity are required, as well as the aid and encouragement of a guide. Then, something most fascinating occurs: what started as a very lonely choice becomes something quite different. One suddenly does not feel alone. To understand this, we must look at the Umbilicum process again. Up to this point, our very dim awareness of the Umbilicum process was composed of the seemingly disconnected glimpses or whispers that filtered through our heavily conditioned minds to our consciousness. Now we begin to realize that our *Areté* beckons to us in the form of Revelation; that is, according to our awareness, what we need is revealed to us. This is a very different world for us, and at first, our steps are quite tentative and need to be encouraged and guided. But soon, we are striding as though born to it, which, of course, we are.

A few more words of pointing to the Umbilicum process are in order here. We could look at it as a repository of species wisdom, but it must be seen as more dynamic, fluid, and encompassing, since there is continuing multiway communication among the

Source, the individual, and others. This communication is absolutely independent of time and space and is in no way limited thereby. The revelation you need at any particular instant may come from a great distance in time and/or space since this realm transcends both of these categories of our Life of Survival. At first, we are hesitant, due to our conditionings, to trust this process, but as we practice, we learn that these revelations can be relied upon. Revelations are not simply for articulating: in fact, they may or may not be expressed or expressible; articulating them generally leads to gross misunderstanding. *Revelations are for acting upon.*

Contrary to popular misconceptions, this new life is not just pensive, and it is neither a separation nor a withdrawing: it is most active and permeates the whole of our lives. In other words, we discover that the Life of Fullness is our true life for which we are meant, transcending yet subsuming our Life of Survival. This is the Soul process that comes to fill our lives through discovering the unique Areté of and by each individual.

There is no "The Way" to follow in a group, but each individual has a unique Path to discover and explore, with the initial aid of a Guide. Then one discovers a true community, based not on derivative Life of Survival values, but on the Soul process in which we come to see one another as Sons or Daughters of God, or as heirs of the Kingdom of Heaven.

Do expressions such as *God* and *Kingdom of Heaven* bother you? (As you can see, I love rescuing concepts and terms from the dungeons of misunderstanding or perversity to which they have been consigned by popular religions and misconception.) *God* and *Kingdom of Heaven* are perfectly good terms for pointing to the Source or the Ultimate and to the Life of the Spirit or the Life of Fullness. These are the eternal basis for a true sense of community.

Eternal is another term that is misused and misunderstood but that can be rescued to aid us in our explorations here. The *eternal* and *eternity* have degenerated in use to refer to time or extensions thereof. *Eternal* has come to be regarded as a synonym for *everlasting*, which is so puerile in meaning but is understandable in terms of the needs of organized religions to coerce uniformity and social control through the promise of an afterlife. The afterlife, by the way, was an incrustation, like so many others, imported into Christianity from earlier mystery religions. Eternity is not a temporal or quantitative concept, but rather a qualitative, nontemporal, nonspatial, transcending concept. As Paul Tillich put it, "Eternity is the invasion of the Now by the Divine." Being Mediterranean rather than Germanic, I would have said it was the "*infusion* of the Now by the Divine," but Tillich expressed it most perceptively because Eternity is a quality of the Now that is manifested or incarnated by the individual who is exploring the Life of Fullness in the everyday world. Jesus promised not everlasting life but Life Eternal if you seek first the Kingdom of Heaven; in other words, a life of bliss or Nirvana when you come to see the true nature of yourself and the Cosmos.

I just said that the Life of Fullness is explored in the everyday world, and this may seem like a contradiction, but that is only apparent. The Life Eternal manifests when we act upon the Life of Fullness or Higher self-order of functioning in the here and now—that is, in this everyday world; but we do not act solely on our everyday conditionings and their derivative values. We have the Umbilicum process and Revelation available to us when we practice accordingly. This is what is meant by "being *in* the world but not *of* it." *In the world* is the only place where we can act in our present form, but we need not be *of* it, which means we need not be limited by the Life of Survival conditionings, values, or worldview.

All of this can seem like an overwhelming task for the individual who must choose it alone, and that is why a Guide is so necessary, at least at first. And it is to the Guide that we now turn.

8

THE GUIDE

*T*his chapter could just as well have been titled "Getting to Feel at Home in No-man's-land and Beyond." Remember that, upon embracing Despair, you turn toward the unknown and enter No-man's-land. This is the stage you find yourself in when you turn away from the exclusive reliance upon your Life of Survival skills and their derivative values and consequently away from the comfort and at-home-ness you normally feel in the everyday-mind approach to life. This is turning away from Man's-land in order to turn toward the transitional stage in which there are no familiar signposts, categories, values, vocabulary, or framework. And since you have become aware of and embraced your Despair, you are without your customary and comforting Hope process, which leaves you vulnerable to the effects of the unalloyed Fear process.

Don't forget that the Hope process evolved for the very purpose of buffering and making tolerable the Fear process, which evolved as society's way of encouraging and enforcing the enculturation process most efficiently. This was needed for successful survival, which in turn is the necessary precondition for making this turn toward the Life of Fullness. This turn toward the unknown requires such an openness on your part that, at least at first, you are vulnerable to the Fear process, whose illusoriness will be discovered in the Second Journey. So, this *appears* to be a catch-22 situation, where you have to transcend the Fear process to start on the Second Journey, but you have to embark on the Second Journey in order to transcend the Fear process. This is why the Guide is so necessary.

As I said, entering this No-man's-land unguided leaves you prey to the effects of the unalloyed Fear process. There are numerous examples of such individuals who attempted to venture forth, relatively untethered to Man's-land, and who, at first, attempted to communicate what they saw through poetry, prose, or other arts. This attempt at communication invariably failed while these people wandered aimlessly and often almost endlessly before succumbing to either madness or suicide. Madness is a social judgment and can be seen as society's verdict on an individual who is no longer considered capable of surviving successfully. Suicide is the individual's verdict that survival is no longer possible or desirable.

As you can see, entering No-man's-land is risk-taking of the highest order, making skydiving, rock-climbing, and bungee-jumping seem like child's play by comparison. This turn toward the Life of Fullness is deceptively similar to the life of the mind in that we use words and concepts to talk about it. But that is where the similarity ends; the words and the concepts *are* the life of the mind, whereas they serve merely as *bridges* to the Life of Fullness. In the life of the mind you are counted as knowing simply for uttering the words and concepts. The Life of Fullness, on the other hand, is much more like a craft, skill, sport, or art. You are counted as knowing not for talking about it, but through the *doing* of it. For example, the concert pianist, the potter, and the carpenter are counted as knowing not for lecturing on, but through the doing of, their art or craft.

So, you can see that this turn to No-man's-land requires more than the thinking and talking about it. Like any craft, skill, sport, or art, a teacher, coach, or guide is necessary to help acquire the skills needed to express your unique gift or talent, in particular here your *Areté*. The skills are those needed for the Second Journey, which includes traversing No-man's-land. The Guide cannot give you the strength and confidence needed for this journey—those are prerequisites that you must have acquired as by-products of successful surviving.

As mentioned earlier, embarking on this Second Journey can be likened to going on safari. A requisite of going on the first safari is the guide who not only guides you over unfamiliar terrain on the journey, but who also helps you to prepare for it. This analogy of the safari guide is quite apt in talking about the Life of Fullness Guide. The most necessary characteristic of the Guide is that he/she has made such a journey before and thus knows firsthand what is involved. Note that I use the more neutral and generic term *Guide* rather than *Teacher* or *Guru*, although these are very appropriate designations except for the many stereotypes that have come to be attached to them, which we might as well avoid here.

Who, then, is the Guide, and from whence does he/she come? The Guide is simply a mutant of this higher consciousness of our emergent human nature. I have already referred to Krishna, Abraham, Gautama, Lao Tsu, Socrates, Jesus, and others as exemplars of this mutation. They were here to show us that this next level of our emergent human nature is available to us. How these mutants are treated by their respective societies is quite interesting. They are invariably not understood by the great majority of people they come into contact with, so that, being such exceptional persons, legends may begin to develop, especially after their death. These legends are invariably misunderstandings and tend to obscure the truth that these mutants manifested or "incarnated," to use another perfectly appropriate old term.

The truth that is incarnated is the result of a grand revelation that the Guide finally chooses to act upon. To understand this, we must realize that the Guide-to-be is a successful survivor of his/her society, with its enculturation well in place when the essentially inexpressible revelation is received. The Guide-to-be becomes aware that he/she is participating in a mystery that is inexplicable in conventional terms. There will be a period of doubt and disbelief during which the Guide-to-be even attempts to deny or ignore the revelation in view of its incompatibility with the then current worldview. Interestingly, documentation of this period in the lives of some Guides, such as Gautama and Jesus, has survived in the legends that have grown about them. In the case of Jesus, this is what the forty days in the wilderness and the three temptations were all about.

Let us here explore those two legends briefly to discover the truths behind them. Obviously, any literal interpretation would miss the mark widely, and we are well aware that any words or expressions in spiritual matters are really pointing at a realm within but beyond the everyday. We must also develop some familiarity with the cultural milieu and idiosyncracies of the languages of that era and society. In those days, the number "forty" was used to denote a rather long time or duration that would exceed ordinary human endurance. Forty days was used when referring to an individual, while forty years would be used in reference to a people or tribe. Wilderness is an ancient and very apt metaphor for No-man's-land. Simply put, Jesus spent a considerable amount of time trying very hard to fit his revelation into the Procrustean bed of his enculturated mind, pitting it against his doubt and disbelief, until he realized the futility of this and the necessity of simply surrendering to and acting on his revelation.

The three temptations were a wonderfully metaphorical and dramatic way of conveying what every Guide-to-be goes through.

This person is a successful survivor, and he/she has various skills that could be employed to go far in that society, which is what is generally encouraged and rewarded. It would be very hard to realize this and not be tempted to take this far easier way out. The Devil is simply a metaphor and a personification of the ever-present process in any society that either a Guide-to-be or a candidate for the Life of Fullness must endure. Being a successful survivor and having skills and abilities that could be used for economic, political, or religious success, the Guide-to-be will be sorely tempted thereby, especially during this wilderness period when nothing else seems to be working.

There is so much of this sort of wisdom and assurance that is available in the scriptures and literature of various traditions, but to use that wonderful saying attributed to Jesus, you must have "the eyes to see and the ears to hear." In other words, the prevalent worldview, the ordinary mind, the conditioned senses will not suffice; you must find new ways of perceiving, going beyond your worldview. Any good textbook on the psychology of perception will show the considerable extent to which we perceive what we expect. Perception is based on our conditioned framework—that is, on conceptions and deceptions, which is what illusions, optical and otherwise, are all about. However, when we become aware of these limits and when we embark on the Second Journey, we open ourselves up to these new ways of seeing and hearing. This is the meaning of finding and using the invisible "third eye," an apt metaphor employed often in some of the spiritual literature.

During the Wilderness period, and after the ever-present temptations to resume the safe, comfortable, conditioned path to earthly rewards, the Guide-to-be comes to the realization that the way out is "surrender." Again, here is a term we encounter frequently in the spiritual literature, usually as "surrendering to God," which can seem so vague or hyperbolic. But this is exactly what the Guide-to-be must do: quit resisting the revelation that has been tendered him/her and surrender to it by acting on it.

This acting on it will fly in the face of the disbelief based upon the enculturated worldview.

It requires great courage here to transcend this conditioning and enter the new world of this revelation. But by being open to and acting on the revelation, the Guide-to-be discovers that it is generative of what may be called divine truth. This divine truth reveals to us who we really are, which contrasts brilliantly with the pale identities we accumulate in our Life of Survival. Knowing who you are is truly an awesome awareness, a continuing unfoldment that is discovered to be the point of our Questing. Knowing who you are is the Soul process, which is practically inexpressible; but you then know who each other human really is and of our relationship to the Source, Cosmos, or God.

At this point, the Guide has gone through the wilderness and is back *in* the world while not being *of* it—that is, not limited to the conditioned framework of the everyday world. Now the Guide is available to those who have the eyes to see and the ears to hear that he/she is the Guide—in other words, available to those who are ready to turn. The Guide has no need to advertise, to hustle, or to develop a following. The Guide simply responds to those who are in need, ready to turn, and recognize him/her. These persons are drawn to the Guide, who in turn is drawn to them. Thus, proselytizing is unnecessary and out of the question, and a large group following is of no interest. The real interest is in true communion or the community of souls, which is to be found in the Life of Fullness and not in the usual groups and organizations.

The Guide may, however, respond to questions of individuals in a group or may attend an interested group for introductory purposes. If there is a group around a Guide, it is usually only an accidental occurrence arising because several individuals happen to be there at the same time. However, the formation of ongoing groups and organizations after the appearance of a Guide is the work of those who failed to act and understand— that is, the failures, the dropouts, and their followers. A case in point are the so-called Apostles of Jesus, none of whom ever evidenced any understanding of his teaching, whereas some other individuals, such as Mary Magdalene, probably grasped and acted on those teachings and thereby found their unique paths.

The Guide, by virtue of the enculturation process, which is not lost or dropped but transcended, will express him-/herself in the vocabulary and framework of that culture, even though the message is universal and timeless. So, we will always have to do some translating when studying a Guide from another time or culture. Each time and culture will have its appropriate Guide or Guides. Some become known; most usually do not. In those few cases when a true Guide becomes known, it is not through the Guide's efforts, but invariably based upon some popular misunderstanding and articulation of the inexpressible.

The Guide's articulations, on the other hand, unless they are introductory or bridging, are intended for a particular individual on the Second Journey who is at some stage of having the eyes to see and the ears to hear. The Guide does not invent a new language, but uses the language of that time and place in a fresh, new way to articulate his/her revelation for the particular individual concerned. Thus, the Guide speaks that which the candidate is ready to hear.

There is an old spiritual saying to the effect that "when the pupil is ready, the teacher appears." This is quite true and would seem magical to most people. We even have a word for this these days—"synchronicity." If you remember that the Umbilicum process is like a multidirectional communicative grid, you can see that, when someone is ready to embark on the Second Journey, this would be communicated in such a way that the Guide and the candidate are brought together in the most improbable of ways.

A great impediment to recognizing the Guide for many potential candidates has always been the *stereotypes of the Guide* under which they labor. In the time of Jesus, we have recorded evidence in the New Testament that even his so-called Apostles and others were continually expecting him to fit some Procrustean stereotype of a messiah, which had a long Judaic tradition (consider especially Judas and Peter). Then Paul came along later and combined such a stereotype with his own experience in Judaism (as Saul) and in the Eastern mystery religions of his frantic search to create the Suffering Servant of the Crucifixion. It is easier to see this in another time.

In our own time, there are also stereotypes of the Guide which hinder. One of them is what I call "the sweet Jesus" type, one who at all times is cloyingly sweet and never raises his voice, as Jesus is certainly reputed to have done when needed. Another of our stereotypes comes from Asia in the form of a Guru or Roshi, usually with a beard, invariably wearing robes, speaking in a charming accent, and generally humorless. I could go on because we have so many such stereotypes from our past or other cultures, but these examples will suffice to point up this impediment. The candidate for the Second Journey will have to transcend his/her enculturation in this also by suspending these stereotypes or else risk missing the appearance of the Guide. Of course, embracing such stereotypes would certainly be an indication that the individual is not yet ready. Let me remind you here that what I have been describing in the foregoing are just some of the stereotypes of the Guide that can be impediments to the Second Journey.

Of course, there are no standard categories for how a Guide looks, speaks, and acts. If we look to the past, we see that the Guide may come from a variety of backgrounds as, for example, royalty in the case of Gautama, the working craftsman class in the case of Jesus, and the citizen-warrior-intellectual in the case of Socrates. In our time, the Guide may have been a businessman, a scientist, a longshoreman, a craftsman, or even a politician, however improbable that seems. How or why a particular person is chosen by the Cosmos to be a Guide is certainly a mystery, which means we can observe and explore even while not understanding. Such understanding is not possible *in* this world while one is still *of* it; such understanding comes only through the Life of Fullness.

The Guide, being not only a successful survivor in his/her society, will also have a breadth and depth of experience in that culture. The candidates for the Second Journey who come to him/her will be from a variety of backgrounds, and the Guide will have to relate his/her revelation in a meaningful way to each one. The Guide is thus a teacher most relevant to his/her time and culture. Each Guide will also exhibit a unique style and practice while revealing the timeless and cosmic message. The Guide is in an extraordinary position as a translator of earlier or other manifestations of the revelation he/she brings. And these always need translating because they are invariably couched in the framework of their time and culture. In this way, the Guide can make meaningful the fragments and mistranslations of earlier teachings we often pick up in our religious conditionings.

The legends and stereotypes that arise about Guides considerably obscure how they work and their relationship to others. Except for introductory and bridging talks, a Guide works primarily with individuals embarking on the Second Journey—to guide them through No-man's-land, and to help find each one's unique path to the Life of Fullness. An excellent analogy comes to us from the world of academia (as it might function ideally). The Guide is like the professor who introduces and educates the student in the subject area to the point where the student can perform independent research, at which point the professor and the student can become colleagues in their work, and eventually they can become peers in their field of inquiry. In similar fashion, the Guide starts out guiding, but fulfillment comes when the candidate becomes a peer, and they can then be coexplorers of this higher realm.

Although teaching can serve here as a good analogy, all analogies have limits, and this one is no exception. This provides me with an opportunity to expand a bit on why I have favored the term *guide* over that of *teacher*. Whether we realize it or not, teaching usually assumes an objectivity, that there is something out there or separate, like a subject matter, to teach. That would be misleading on the Second Journey, where the central process is discovery—primarily to discover who you really are. This cannot be taught or communicated by any teacher, but can only be discovered within. I have often used a more precise word for emphasis: the Second Journey is a *heuristic* process—that is, learning through discovering by doing. Further, although it is rarely remembered, the term *educate* comes from the Latin *educare*, meaning to draw out or forth (from within). Thus, we can see that the Guide is the true educator.

Implicit in all of this is that the Guide is also a learner and a discoverer: actually, the Guide learns the most in this process of guiding and exploring. So, the Guide works to eliminate the need for him-/herself as Guide in each individual candidate, as well as working to disabuse each one of any tendency to worship or treat the Guide as anything but a learned peer. As coexplorers, they will each be on unique paths discovering different facets and principles of this realm which they can share. This is the new and true community of our emergent human nature, based upon the inward discovery of our Oneness rather than on the superficial, external, commonly held goals and purposes of organizations and so-called communities that have failed us in the past. *Community* and *communion* have the same root, meaning coming into union or, better yet and more accurately, recognizing our Oneness. And that can only happen when you discover your Soul process or who you really are, which entails your relationship to the Cosmos in the Life of Fullness.

There is an almost always unexpected characteristic of the Guide, and that is a sense of humor. To have lived life as fully as a Guide-to-be does would drive the ordinary person to cynicism or to some existential sense of "no exit," while in the Guide the disproportionality of human effort and outcome seems cartoon-like and leads to a well-developed sense of humor as a means of living with the disingenuousness of most people. The Guide incorporates this sense of humor in his/her teaching efforts, which is best exemplified and preserved in the Sufi tradition by the Tales of Nasrudin. Usually, this characteristic of a Guide who becomes widely known is not preserved in the literature because those who did such preserving rarely understood the Guide and were often humorless functionaries of an institution organized to achieve social control and cohesion.

It is quite a miracle that the Tales of Nasrudin survive. (By the way, Nasrudin is not believed to be any single individual but rather a composite of legends of many Guides, each one taking a different guise depending on the point of the story; the Tales have their roots in very old oral traditions.) I am not aware of anything comparable that survives in the Christian tradition of the West. Although humor can be found in the literature of Zen and some other spiritual traditions, it is rare.

Most often, what survives in the literature of a tradition is a caricature of the Guide and of some original utterances. Such caricatures are not worth following and would, of course, be misleading. Only the Guide and the Umbilicum process can guide. The Guide's efforts are directed at leading the candidate to learn from the Source through the Umbilicum process—that is, from the Inner Guide—so that the Guide is no longer needed as Guide. When the Guide dies, he/she can no longer guide in the world, except through the Umbilicum process. Thus, attempts at preserving the words of a Guide are so often misleading; the words of a Guide are intended for the particular candidate to whom they are addressed. As has been said, there is a unique relationship between the teacher, the teaching, and the taught, and that changes even if it appears that the same words are uttered to a different candidate.

Just before this, I was discussing a sense of humor as an unexpected characteristic of the Guide, but I did not reveal its true source, only the preconditions of the Guide's experience in this world. Actually, what occurs is that the Guide, in the process of exploring the Life of Fullness, discovers something quite remarkable. We have a simple word to point at it, but it will not be meaningful until the candidate makes it his/her own discovery. What can be discovered is quite simply that the Cosmos is at *Play.* This is not easy to grasp, and, of course, understanding can come only when you make it your own discovery. But we can point at it somewhat here.

Play must be distinguished from what we call games. A game has a set framework, rules, and fixed goals, and this is what most people erroneously think of as Play. Once past early childhood and well into enculturation, people become almost constitutionally unable to Play again, except briefly on rare occasions—such as under the influence of drugs, licit or illicit—and even then it eventuates into games under the strong influence of our enculturation. Play has no goals, rules, or a set framework and is done for its own sake or as an outward expression of inward joy. If you want to see the closest thing to Play, watch a small child or children "at play" before they have learned the stylized games of their culture.

Instead of the grim business that nearly everyone construes as life, the Guide comes to see that the Cosmos is actually always at Play, and the Guide, in becoming aware of and surrendering to the Source, comes to emulate the Cosmos. Of course, what the great majority of people take very seriously in this life becomes a rich source of humor for the Guide. But as you can discover from dealing with teenagers, for example, a sense of humor about a subject is possible only after it has been taken seriously, pursued to its limits, and then taken beyond those limits. It is only then that we can laugh at it, not before. Similarly, when the Guide and the candidate have gone beyond taking the Life of Survival so seriously as if it were the whole of Life and have transcended to the Life of Fullness, they discover that the Cosmos is at Play. They cannot again take too seriously the Life of Survival, which becomes for them a rich source of humor. This is why the Guide and the candidate who has transcended to the Life of Fullness will always tend to Play. And this is what the Tales of Nasrudin are really expressing.

Explaining the Guide can be no more satisfactorily done than explaining Michelangelo, Da Vinci, Bach, Mozart, Copernicus, Newton, or Einstein, all of whom were also mutants of the third level, appealing to those who had the eyes to see and the ears to hear at the third or creating the harmonizing/aesthetic level of awareness. Each of these mutants in his own unique way was pointing at the harmony that he glimpsed of the Cosmos through the gift or talent that came to him through the Umbilicum process. The Guide also receives a gift in the form of Revelation through the Umbilicum process, but his/her guiding is based not upon a glimpse but upon what can best be described as a face-to-face continuing encounter with the Source, which the candidate is then encouraged and aided to realize.

9

THE PRACTICE — WHY

The Guide receives, as an integral part of his/her grand revelation, a *Practice* to aid those who are ready to turn and embark on the Second Journey. The Practice is a new basis for acting *in* the world while not being *of* it. It is, in turn, based upon a framework and vocabulary that bridge our enculturation and the Life of Fullness, or that bridge our Lower self-order of functioning and our Higher self-order of functioning. The Practice, together with its framework and vocabulary, is essential for embarking on the Second Journey, but is of no use to anyone who has not made certain claims (these claims have been discussed earlier as prerequisites to this journey).

The first prerequisite or claim that must be made is that you have discovered and reached the limits of successful survival or of the third level of awareness. Second, you must be aware of your Despair. Third, you must then embrace your Despair. The fourth claim involves your turning from an exclusive reliance upon your conditioned worldview and mind-set and simultaneously turning toward the unknown realm of the Second Journey. Last, you must claim the Guide. This last claim may not occur fully in a flash but may unfold over time as you develop the eyes to see and the ears to hear through the Practice.

In order to see why a Practice is necessary, you must first understand some elements of how our conditioning works. First, we need to distinguish between reacting and responding. In actual situations, people generally act on their reactions—that is, unreflectively and based upon their past conditioning, quite automaton-like. The apparent exceptions to this are situations like the workplace or the military, for example, where people are acting under some overarching directive that is coercive; this is simply behavior modification, relatively voluntary or involuntary, as under conscription. In such situations, people seem to have overcome their reactions, but actually, all that has happened is that their behavior has been modified to *react* in a new way that is more appropriate to the requirements of the imposing organization or agency. So, we still end up with reacting as the primary mode.

As people develop the ability to reflect, the result of the mental, affective, and behavioral training that we call education, they become able to transcend their reactions and then learn to respond. It is not that the conditioned, automatic reactions cease, but rather that the reflective individual has learned not to act on them. This is a development in human evolution that is usually not sufficiently appreciated. Without this development, civilization would not have been possible, not to mention its foundation of continued, assured successful survival, so necessary as a precondition for the Second Journey.

Learning not to act on our reactions was quite a development, involving delaying gratification, which in turn required the creation of a concept of time. This probably started in our evolution during our early hunting and gathering days, when we developed strategies and cooperation, both of which require not acting on reactions, as well as delaying immediate gratification.

The success experienced in the hunt must have been sought elsewhere in human activities, necessitating similar strategies and cooperation. This ability not to act on our reactions, and consequently to reflect, had great survival value; this became the mark of the mature human, but it was the result of a long enculturation process that to this day has quite mixed results. So many people never seem to get to this stage in their lives, or do so very unevenly so that some areas of their lives are practically untouched.

Please note that not acting upon our reactions does not mean that we cease to have them. We continue having the reactions, including any associated expletives, but we do not just automatically act upon them. (This is an important distinction for us that will be clarified later.) Thus, not acting upon our reactions and attaining the ability to reflect are the prerequisites to what I call *responding*. As we shall see, this is the ability to act based on choiceless awareness rather than acting upon our more automatic reactions. This is acting by choice, which is responding.

There is a kind of law of conservation that applies to our conditioning, whether it is mental, affective, or behavioral. We may be able to change any of these superficially or briefly, but in sticky, difficult, or extreme situations, the old conditioning resumes and emerges triumphant. Further, the mental conditioning is the easiest to change, while the affective and behavioral are much more resistant. How many people read books or hear lectures on diet or self-improvement, for example, emerge convinced with a new way of thinking, perhaps even change briefly or superficially, but then remain essentially their old selves?

Changing mental conditioning is relatively easy compared to changing affective and behavioral conditionings. On very rare occasions, these can be changed by some extreme or life-threatening situation, but even then we tend to return to "the evil we know." Do not forget that, as successful survivors, we know that our conditionings are most efficacious for survival, and we have a great stake in conserving them. We can even get to the point where we are convinced thoroughly mentally, but in actual situations, our affective and behavioral conditionings overcome us, and we return to our safe, enculturated ways. Yet we now know that these ways, while necessary for our continued successful survival, will interfere with what is needed for the Second Journey.

At this point, it appears that you have to choose between successful survival and the Second Journey, and yet the Second Journey requires your continued successful survival. Is this another catch-22? No—you must become "amphibious," a concept introduced for this sort of context by Aldous Huxley in his remarkable book *The Perennial Philosophy*. Being amphibious means being able to function fully and equally well in two different media, including, but not limited to, land and water. In our context, amphibious relates to the two realms: the Life of Survival and the Life of Fullness. The Life of Survival continues during our Second Journey. So for us, the term amphibious also implies a simultaneity, transcending not only space, but time as well.

Although it is your Yearning that calls you to the Second Journey, you must use your mind to discover the limits of the First Journey and then to embark on the Second Journey. First, we require bridging concepts, categories, and a framework to make the transition and to point to the inexpressible realm of the Life of Fullness. These concepts, categories, and framework may even be quite successful in changing your mind—that is, in changing your mental conditioning—but they alone will falter in changing your affective and behavioral conditioning. This is why the Guide and the Practice are so necessary. Your affective and behavioral conditionings are quite resistant to the effects of mental conditioning. They need stronger medicine to go along with the new mental conditioning.

What is needed is a new way of acting in the world that will accomplish two ends: first, you must be able to inhibit the old mental, affective, and behavioral conditioning, and second, you must become open to learning what works in the new realm of our Second Journey. This cannot be accomplished by mental conditioning alone, as necessary as it is as a precondition. You must go beyond it, to conditioning that opens you up to the unknown. Now, this may sound paradoxical, but in this world where you will apply the Practice as a successful survivor, conditioning is overcome or superseded only by new conditioning.

The difference between this new conditioning and the old is great and qualitative. The aim of the old conditioning was control and closure. As discussed earlier, we seek control over our entire environment, including ourselves and others. We also tend to seek conclusions, climaxes, and closure on experiences. The new conditioning of the Practice has quite different needs and aims. First, you are seeking an openness to this new realm, an openness which requires the ability to inhibit selectively the old conditionings when they are not specifically needed for survival. Second, you require the ability to suspend your inclination to control, when not specifically needed for your survival, so that you can be open to and discover your true Power in this new realm.

But how can you go about this task of changing your worldview—your consciousness? This will require a twofold learning process. Now, let us remember that you need much of your Life of Survival conditionings so that you can continue surviving successfully as the required base for the Second Journey. First, whatever you do must have the effect of inhibiting by choice the old behavioral, affective, and mental conditionings that are not necessary for successful survival and that work as impediments to the Second Journey. Second, what you do must also have the effect of taking you to the threshold where you can begin to explore the Life of Fullness and discover who you really are. In the past, this has been attempted quite often, by people placing themselves under the control of another individual or some organization. For reasons already amply discussed earlier, this does not work; nor do leaps of faith or choices made in an emotional thrall that leave our reflective intellect behind.

Further, this herculean task must be accomplished through a Practice that is both *simple* and *comprehensive*. This means that the Practice must be simple enough to be readily learned mentally in such a way that the mental component in any new situation or event is minimal; thus, the emphasis can be on retraining the more resistant affective and behavioral components that are the impediments. You see, mentally accepting or affirming an idea or concept is only a prelude and not a substitute for acting on it as a whole person. Further, as we shall see, such acting on it requires the integration of all three dimensions: the mental, behavioral, and affective. Finally, the Practice must be comprehensive enough to be applicable to any new situation or event.

Remember, working toward this new realm is deceptively similar to the life of the mind in that we use words and concepts to talk about it or point to it, but that is where the similarity ends. This realm is much more like a craft, skill, sport, or art, in that you are counted as knowing not through utterances about it but through the doing of it. Further, the aim of the Practice is not to make you a perfect practitioner; its aim is to transcend itself to the process of Enlightenment, the Kingdom of Heaven, Nirvana, or Salvation (that is, being saved from such a limited and stunted life), whichever way you like to point at the ineffable Life of Fullness. But the Practice is as necessary as any practice in a sport, skill, art, or craft; that is, to eliminate the many acquired blocks and inhibitions to the expression of your natural talents or gifts, this being the highest and latest gift of your emergent human nature.

The Practice is needed to overcome the conditioned successful survival impediments to which we become habituated, and then practically addicted, as if the Life of Survival were the whole of life. Without the Practice, you would simply continue on your enculturated dead-end path with, at most, occasional misguided mental, affective, or behavioral eruptions that cannot be generative. The mental, affective, and behavioral must be integrated into a Practice in order to transcend your everyday life and thus avert the ennui that awaits if you endure only the First Journey.

IO

THE PRACTICE—WHAT

The Practice itself is eminently practical; that is, it must actually be lived. Simply reading and memorizing the elements of the Practice, although necessary preliminaries, will not be sufficient for embarking on the Second Journey. The Practice consists of *acting on* what appear to be answers to four very basic life questions. These four questions are not only fundamental, they are quite simple:

1. Who am I?
2. Why am I here?
3. Where am I?
4. What am I to do?

The answers offered are also quite simple and function so that if you act on them, then at least your existing conditionings that are impediments in this area are inhibited. Further, the answers to these questions may be treated as four tentative hypotheses to be tested—that is, acted upon—in your everyday world; in this way, you will thus be able to verify them because they are so generative. The questions and their respective answers are as follows.

1. *Who am I?* "I am a *son/daughter* (depending on gender) of God." For those of you who find the term *God* a difficulty, you may use the less-charged term *Cosmos*. The important theme here is to overcome the conditioning of which you are often unaware: that you are only an unimportant iteration or member of a species who is practically interchangeable with others. This conditioning also makes you highly dependent upon the feedback of others for a sense of identity. Such identities are what you must learn to transcend. Identities, such as names or titles— like husband or wife, professor, officer, physician, artist, star, or mother of the year—are really just labels. We tend to identify with these labels, and yet we never confuse the label with the contents of a jar.

Further, these labels or identities can be quite transitory and changeable, telling you nothing about, as well as serving to obscure, who you really are. Who you really are can be discovered only in the Life of Fullness and not through any feedback from other people, no matter how exalted they appear. Acting on the answer to this question helps you go beyond your conditioned identities so that you can be open to who you really are. Remember that these are only words and bridging concepts that point toward transcending your everyday mind or worldview.

Being a son/daughter of God is intended to convey a sense of importance to you; importance not in comparison with others, but importance in comparison with your existing sense of self, which is based on transient identities and is very dependent on psychosocial feedback. By acting on the answer to the question "Who am I?" you not only will be in the process of discovering who you are, you will also inescapably be discovering who each other person is: a son/daughter of God. The difficulty here is that the great majority of others will not have arrived at such aware-ness and will still be caught up in the world of illusion. However, their unawareness does not change the reality of which you will have become aware. Encountering other people will have much of the quality of encountering a brother or sister who is suffering from amnesia. Or, to put it as succinctly as I have had to on numerous occasions: "The only difference between you and me is that I know who you really are!"

Also intended here is a new view of your relationship with God or the Cosmos; namely, the relationship of *heir*. Note that an heir does not have to earn, but simply makes a claim to, that inheri-tance. What you are heir to is really quite inexpressible, except to say you can discover who you really are—your Higher self-order of functioning. Also included in the concept of heir is that you share the qualities or characteristics of God or the Cosmos. But you can discover these only in action. With words, all you can do is point at it: by acting on this answer, you have the opportunity of discovering and incarnating the truth of who you are.

2. *Why am I here?* "I am here to let my unique Divine Plan unfold." This is a simple statement that is loaded with meaning. First, let me say that this is not referring to some grand overall "Divine Plan" for all. This refers to "*my* unique Divine Plan." An excellent analogy here is that of your very unique genetic plan. This genetic plan is not a blueprint, but a set of potentials which may or may not be realized depending on how our lives are lived. Deprivations (such as vitamin C deficiency), accidents (such as loss of limb), disease (such as diabetes), and various misen-culturations or malenculturations (such as childhood abuse) can seriously limit the fulfillment of these potentials. Contrariwise, having the opportunities and acting on them can enhance and fulfill these potentials. Similarly, your unique Divine Plan is not a blueprint, but is like a set of potentials which may or may not be realized. Like the genetic plan, these are unique for each one of us. Unlike the genetic plan, which is limited primarily to your

body and somewhat to your mind, the Divine Plan, while also concerned with your body and mind, is especially concerned with your Soul process, which is the emergent human nature that you are here to discover and explore.

Note the words *let* and *unfold*. These are intended to convey something quite different from our tendency to "make it happen," which is also the way of the ubiquitous self-improvement programs (which are fine for the Life of Survival). No, you cannot *make* your unique Divine Plan *happen*, but you can *let* it *unfold*. *Unfold* here conveys the sense of being revealed. Revelation is simply the response of the Source, God, or the Cosmos to your Yearning through the Umbilicum process. Other words for your unique Divine Plan are your *Fullness* or your *Areté*.

You can discover, by acting on this answer to the second question, that letting your unique Divine Plan unfold entails primarily getting yourself—that is, your Lower self-order of functioning—out of the way. In other words, you will discover that you have spent most of your life interfering with and preventing the unfolding of your unique Divine Plan. Although many are necessary for successful survival, most of your Life of Survival conditionings have the effect of buffering or interfering with your unique Divine Plan. All you need to do is to claim it and who you are, as an heir would claim a throne or a fortune, which pales in comparison to your birthright—your unique Divine Plan.

3. *Where am I?* "I am in God's good world where all runs according to principle such that each next event is the will of God." God's good world is a message that permeates so much of the spiritual literature, and it may even sound redundant to some to combine "God" and "good." But here we are trying to counter the effects of the experiences people have when they are limited to acting on their conditioned-for-survival Lower self-order of functioning. This is what has been referred to as "man's will" or our "willfulness," as compared to surrendering to God's will. So

many of these expressions tend to be turnoffs or confusing unless they are related to a generative framework, which is what we are doing here.

Assuming that you are a successful survivor, using your Lower self-order of functioning conditionings for anything other than survival will not work or be generative. Whenever that failure is encountered, it is often interpreted as a shortcoming or flaw of the Cosmos, when the shortcoming is actually in our conditioning. This can soon degenerate to a view of the Cosmos as uncaring or indifferent or even hostile. If we persisted in trying to milk a cow by pumping its tail, should we blame the cow for not producing? So, the prevailing belief (except for those who still have magical or childish religious beliefs) of so many intelligent people that we live in at best an indifferent and at worst a hostile world or Cosmos needs to be countered. That is why you need to claim and act on the truth that is pointed at by the expression "God's good world."

The next phrase in our answer is "where all runs according to principle." This counters the conditioned view that is embraced by so many people that anything beyond our readily controllable world of survival is quite beyond us and probably part of a helter-skelter or magical reality. Many otherwise intelligent people tend to this view even in the face of our discoveries of the last several centuries that have demonstrated over and over again that all runs according to principle. I am talking about the innumerable probings of our world by scientists, engineers, and others whenever we have quit viewing a particular set of phenomena as subject to magic or helter-skelter and then gone on to discover that these phenomena actually were according to principle.

Such fields as chemistry, physics, geology, psychology, and biology, not to mention numerous others, have investigated phenomena previously believed to be subject to magic, incantation, evil spirits, or appeasable gods. Invariably, these phenomena were discovered to be the operation of principle. This has been going on long enough and so extensively that I find it amazing that any intelligent person can still hold such childishly religious or magical views and not see the principled orderliness that governs the Cosmos even in matters we have not yet explored appropriately.

"Such that each next event is the will of God" is a corollary of the previous phrase but not as readily grasped. If the Cosmos runs according to principle, then all phenomena are the expression of principle or principles. Unless we hold to a magical or childish anthropomorphic view of the will of God, we can see that these expressions of principle are what is meant by the "will of God," which is a fine shorthand expression for this larger understanding. Remember now that this has to be claimed, just as a tentative hypothesis has to be grasped and then acted on, in order to discover the truth of it.

4. *What am I to do?* Nothing will change for you if all you do is mentally grasp the foregoing. There must be a basis or framework for acting on these answers in your everyday world or consciousness so that you can transform your view of reality to accord with that of the Cosmos. The answer to the question "What am I to do?" is more complex and has two basic components: the *Inward* and the *Outward*. The Inward is seemingly the simpler, but can be the more difficult due to some serious misconceptions that abound. The Inward component is "going for *Meditation*," but to grasp what that is, you must approach it most innocently—that is, without any of the usual preconceptions.

Meditation is not anything you can do; that is, no human has ever meditated. What you can do is to *"go for* Meditation"; this is a critical distinction, which, if not appreciated, leads to the intense frustration, deceptions, or illusions that have been experienced by the many who have tried "to meditate." There is a wonderfully apt analogy for going for Meditation, and that is going for massage. When you go for massage, nothing is required of you but to present yourself without the encumbrance of your clothing and to relax. You do not *do* anything: the massage is done to you.

In going for Meditation, you must also relax and present yourself unencumbered by any of the garments of your conditioned goals, expectations, or stereotypes. You are not to bring an agenda or menu. Just simply present yourself quietly and with choiceless awareness; that is, let the Meditation be done unto you by the Source. You must get out of the way so that you may receive these true nutrients of the Spirit. Getting out of the way means that you cease your ordinary ways of always trying to control your world and your self. Going for Meditation is to be done alone and quietly—that is, without the distractions of others and of the clamoring sensory world.

Let us clear up some prevalent confusions here. Achieving tranquility or "getting into alpha" is not Meditation. However, a tranquil state may be a very helpful precondition for Meditation, but choiceless awareness is what is necessary. Nor is chanting or prayer to be confused with Meditation. These are often mistakenly and misguidedly recommended to be used as aids to take your mind off the everyday; but then your mind is occupied with the chant or the prayer, which then acts as a buffer between you and the Source. Any such buffers must be avoided because they interfere with becoming aware of your Oneness with the Source, the point of going for Meditation.

Of course, your everyday mind is not competent in Meditation, and it is impossible to make it blank, as is sometimes earnestly urged by the misguided. It is really simpler and more straightforward to take your mind off the everyday by just reducing the sensory inputs, by being alone, and by neither resisting nor entertaining the thoughts that come. Let them come and simply pass through; just do not entertain them. I even recommend taking a pad and pen along to make note of errands and things that come to mind that need doing so that you are not distracted for the entire session trying so hard to remember any of these. Further, nothing sensory, affective, behavioral, or mental that occurs during a session is any part of Meditation, whether it is an image, a feeling, or a thought, although Meditation will certainly come to influence your thoughts, feelings, actions, and worldview in a most amazing and mysterious way.

All you need in order to go for Meditation is your awareness of the Yearning, which is quite unavoidable since that is what has brought you to this stage. This, together with your naked Intent (which will be explained in the next chapter)—and by presenting yourself innocently or like a little child in wonder, with choiceless awareness—is going for Meditation. Meditation does not take place in time, but you may require from five to fifteen minutes, sometimes more, to achieve the just-mentioned preconditions, which will take less time with practice. This needs to be done upon arising from sleep and just before retiring for the day, as well as at least one other time during the day. Beyond the minimum three times daily, you should do it as often as you can without interfering with successful survival. Going for Meditation is the Cosmic or spiritual nutrition needed for the energy required for the Second Journey.

The Outward component of the answer to "What am I to do?" consists of two elements to be performed *sequentially in any next event* in your everyday world until they become habitual. These are *Let* and *Love*. Again, please get rid of any preconceptions regarding these terms. They are old words that we will be using in quite new ways in accord with this new framework, just as is done in science with terms such as *mean* in statistics, *charm* in theoretical physics, or *fault* in geology.

First, *Let* means "choiceless awareness" in any next event, but acting upon it is not easy. In any next event, which is defined as *an event in which you have a choice to make*, your stance must be one of choiceless awareness, which means being aware of the situation in that next event without the usual overlay of your goals and purposes. Otherwise, as is normal, as well as being well documented in the field of the psychology of perception, your goals and purposes color and distort your awareness. You must practice looking at any next event or situation choicelessly or without your usual mindset. In other words, *you need to perceive and receive each next event as though you had no stake in the outcome.*

Second, after assuming the stance of Let, you need to Love, which means "to respond according to the needs of the situation." This simple statement requires considerable explication, and we shall examine it in reverse order of the wording. The "situation" referred to involves each next event, which you recall includes only events in which you have a choice to make. Whether you have a choice to make is contextual and not determined only by the externals of the event. For example, hearing and/or seeing an airplane flying overhead are not a next event unless you are, for example, an aircraft spotter during World War II. Further, the situation or larger context of a next event may include elements or circumstances that are not immediately present in time or space. For example, the report of a dramatic decline in the stock market could be a next event for you if you had recently purchased stock or if someone quite close to you, but not present, had just purchased stock. So the next event may have connections in other times and other places that must be included in the situation.

Note that I am talking about the "needs," not the "wants," of the situation. Discerning needs from wants is something every parent learns and must learn, not that this is the only way we learn this discernment, but we can use parenting as an excellent analogy here. In the process of raising children, and not through courses or reading books, parents learn to discern needs from wants. An example would be of a little boy who has been put to bed but who later cries out "I need a glass of water." This may or may not be need for water based on thirst. It may actually be a desire or want to stay up longer or simply a want or need for the company and comfort of the parent. In any case, a parent soon learns to discern needs from wants in the process of parenting.

Likewise, you will be learning to discern needs from wants in the process of Practicing.

"According" to the needs means bringing about harmony (as in "accord") among potentially conflicting needs. In any given situation, you will often face needs that conflict, including not only the needs of others but also your own needs. Nothing here should be construed as putting either the needs of others or of yourself first. That can only be determined contextually through Practicing.

Again, let us use an analogy here from parenting in order to illustrate "according to the needs of the situation." You are a young mother with an infant who is crying in the crib. You surmise that the infant is probably hungry, and you pick it up and feed it. But suppose now as you pick the baby up, you determine that the diaper is loaded and very wet. You would now respond by changing its diaper first and then feeding it. Now suppose the very same situation but that also you need to go to the bathroom urgently. You would first go to the bathroom, then change the baby's diaper, and then feed it. Now let us add a further variable: the crib is on fire! You would first extinguish or deal with the fire, insuring the safety of the baby, you, and your home, then go to the bathroom, then change the diaper, and finally, you would feed the baby. This may seem like an oversimplified analogy, but it does represent the principle underlying our concept of "according." In any situation, you need to establish priority among needs and to harmonize them. As with the parenting analogy, this is not learned from books or courses but by experience or Practicing in the world.

Now we turn to the important term *respond* because it is critical that you *respond* rather than act on your reactions. These terms and the distinction between them have already been discussed in the previous chapter, and I recommend going back over that section at this point. Also, let me add here a practical suggestion that will help you in learning to respond. Remember, it is not that you cease having reactions; that is impossible. What you need to learn to do is to "catch" the reaction in each next event; that is, you must *pause momentarily* upon perceiving that next event and not just act on the reaction automatically, no matter how long you have been doing it that way. This brief pause is what you need in order to remember to Practice. Thus, you can truly act by choice, and that is responding.

Love, in order to be realized in its fullness, must eventually be universalized. Cosmic or Divine Love would exclude nothing, so we need a concept to reflect that. Such a concept that is quite old in usage and that needs our rescuing is *Stewardship*, which describes our true relationship to all things, living or not, in our world. So far, in describing Love as I have, you could easily misunderstand me as limiting it to other people only or, in a flourish of generosity, to include all sentient beings. No, Love is not so restricted or constrained; it applies to all, whether sentient or not, including all of the "things" in our world.

To grasp this, you must remember that *Areté* applies not just to humans, but also to all living and nonliving entities: everything in all of creation has a fullness or excellence to express. This applies not only to our children, relatives, friends, cats, dogs, and other animals, but also, for example, to our houses, clothing, furniture, tools, stereos, vehicles, property, plants, and trees. Thus, Stewardship describes your relationship with any entity which has been placed in your care, even if temporarily, whether through purchase, loan, gift, birth, finding, or however encountered; it requires that you attend to the *Areté* of that entity. It is almost needless to say that you would not, if you had in the past, treat animals, houses, furniture, stereos, vehicles, and such as "just things" any longer. And you would be astonished at how such things and animals, not to mention persons, respond to Stewardship.

Acting on Stewardship expands your awareness of your capacity for Love. Such Love is a dynamic in which you find yourself more than just rewarded. You will discover the Unity or that Oneness with all. I could get quite specific, such as how full your relationships with others or pets become, or how fully and much longer your cars, stereos, tools, and other implements serve you, but I think it is much more fun, astonishing, and delightful for you to discover this in each case individually and personally.

This Love that has been described here, if you dwell on it a bit, is really the greatest love imaginable, making that sentimental version of your conditioning seem so limited and unworthy of who you really are. Could any grander love be imagined than one in which *you* are responded to according to the needs of your situation? That is how you are loved by the Source or God. It is the best human expression and approximation of Divine Love, and this is what you are here to practice and embody on the Second Journey.

To sum up the elements of the Practice, you must learn to act on the answers to the four basic life questions: Who am I? Why am I here? Where am I? and What am I to do? The answers to these questions are, respectively: (1) I am a son/daughter of God; (2) I am here to let my unique Divine Plan unfold; (3) I am in God's good world where all runs according to principle such that each next event is the will of God; (4) The Inward component of what to do is going for Meditation, and the Outward component consists of two elements: *Let*, or choiceless awareness, and *Love*, which is responding according to the needs of the situation. So, in each next event, your stance must be choiceless awareness, and your action or response must be choiceful Love.

Your first task is to read, grasp, and then to memorize the four parts of the Practice. That task is preliminary to the most important task of acting on the four parts in a *coordinated* manner until your actions become an integrated whole, and that is to Practice. As you can see, although the Practice is really quite simple, it is far, far from easy, but you will have all the help you need in the Yearning, your *Areté*, and the Umbilicum process, together with the Guide.

However, the Practice as given so far is incomplete without the critical foundational element to which we will now turn.

II

THE PRACTICE—THE INTENT AND HOW, WHEN, WHERE

*T*he foregoing description of the Practice can enable you to grasp it, but remember that knowing or understanding can come only with the doing. I use the term *grasp* to signify the necessary, but not sufficient, requirement of just mentally comprehending something, whereas in this realm, as in a craft, sport, skill, or art, you cannot be considered as *knowing* unless you then can also *do* the Practice. The aim here is to make the Practice habitual, or the new conditioning, so that you can inhibit, when needed, the inappropriate and interfering old conditioning and consequently be open to Revelation of the unknown.

You could attempt to act on the Practice as set forth so far and yet not get anywhere on the Second Journey. To grasp this, you may find an analogy helpful. Let us look at the four elements (the four questions and their answers) of the Practice as the four corners of a structure you are building. Each of the four corners is most important to the building—your Practice—but without a proper foundation, the structure cannot be built nor would it reliably stand. The foundation to which I refer, and without which the Practice is fruitless, is what I call your *Intent*.

This Intent must be desireless, and it is essential for the Practice. To put this into words is most difficult; again, I will use some very old words in a rather new way, so please approach this without prejudice or preconception. Your Intent must be to "Yearn first for the Kingdom of Heaven." Yearning for the Kingdom of Heaven is actually redundant because what else is the Yearning about but your *Areté*, the Higher self-order of functioning, the Kingdom of Heaven, Union with the One, or Nirvana, all of which are simply ways of pointing at that ineffable Life of Fullness.

What needs to be stressed here is the phrase "Yearn first." Now that you are aware of your Yearning, it becomes critical that you then claim its priority in your life. So, *first* is not being used as a temporal term but rather as an ontological term stressing priority; your Intent must be prior in importance to, or come before any of, your goals and purposes in this world. Thus, your Intent is very simply the requisite next step after becoming aware of the Yearning; this is what makes it truly possible to embrace your Despair. The Yearning must be at the very center of your life. Make it the focus of your being. This centering or focusing of your Yearning is the necessary condition for embarking on the Second Journey and for making the Practice efficacious.

However, in your conditioning, there is a great impediment to such a centering or focusing of your Yearning, and this I call *Attachment*. Attachment exists any time that anything, including a goal, a purpose, or a relationship, has priority over Yearning for the Kingdom of Heaven. Obviously then, life before the Second Journey can only be one of Attachment. In reaction to this and subsequent exposure to some of the spiritual literature, some people will attempt "detachment." This is not only an error, even if well intended; it is impossible. Detachment assumes that there is something real to which you are attached and from which you are to be detached.

Attachment is an illusory condition and conditioning. Let us look here at the term *illusory* and realize that the illusion resides neither in the perceiver nor in the object of perception, but rather in the relationship between the two. I call attachment illusory because it describes a *relationship* between the individual and the object or goal or purpose in question that is unreal and erroneous, though conditioned. The difficulty here is not with the objects, goals, or purposes, but in your relationship to them and their priority.

You see, the Intent to Yearn first for the Kingdom of Heaven is not really a goal or purpose to strive for; it is the truth or reality of our emergent human nature of which you can become aware on the Second Journey, through the Practice. There is no need to detach from an illusion, but only to see that it is illusory. Attachment is illusory because it involves a deception that is conditioned in us. The deception is that anything can claim priority over the Kingdom of Heaven. Just because a deception is not discovered or takes a long time to be discovered does not make it any less a deception. It is through the Practice that you can discover the deception that is behind the illusoriness of attachment. This discovery process in the Practice leads you to see that our natural state is not detachment, but one of *Nonattachment*.

So, your Intent transcends your goals and purposes but does not erase them. There is nothing inherently wrong with pursuing any of your goals and purposes, as long as the Yearning comes first. If your Intent is at the center of your life, then the Practice can be generative.

The Practice, based upon your Intent and aided by a Guide, will enable you to traverse No-man's-land safely and begin your explorations of the Life of Fullness on the Second Journey. The Practice involves very concrete actions in the world; in each next event, you need to act on the four answers to the four fundamental questions. This is not easy at first, but actually quite awkward; like learning to ride a bicycle or to swim, it involves *coordination*. As with swimming, bicycling, or any skill, do not expect to coordinate acting on all four answers smoothly at first. In any particular next event, you may find yourself focusing on acting on one of the answers more than on the others. That is fine and no problem; as with swimming, the coordination of acting on all four together will come with practice. Furthermore, acting on this new framework will confound and surprise your Lower self-order of functioning awareness. Remember, it is only the Lower self-order of functioning that is in need of Practicing, and it is the one realm in which we can exercise control. So, paradoxically, you will use control to overcome your controlling ways.

People who just talk about, read books on, and go to lectures on spiritual matters are, to use my favorite analogy for this, much like the person who wants to learn how to swim *before* getting into the water. Obviously, you must get into the water in order to discover that it can be trusted to hold you up; only then is learning to swim possible. The Second Journey—begun by the Practice, not the talking, lectures, or books—is the analog for the water here. Practicing is the getting into the water—the acting on, rather than only listening to or talking and reading about spiritual matters; these latter endeavors can be preliminary to the Second Journey, but they are not sufficient. You must act—Practice.

Unlike quests in most religious traditions and in so much of the spiritual literature, the Second Journey does not require faith as it is usually conceived; namely, as a long-term operation or condition needed to overcome doubt and reason, continually in need of shoring-up. What is required is a much simpler and more short-term *Trust that the Cosmos or Source will hold you up*, rather like the water in our swimming analogy. And that Trust is needed for just the brief period of time it takes for you to act and discover in the Practice that the Cosmos can be trusted.

Such Trust is rather similar to that the scientist has in the orderliness of whatever universe he/she is investigating and acting in—a practically universal and unquestioned basic assumption of all scientific inquiry. Further, there is no need on the Second Journey to overcome doubt and reason. These are to be regarded as respected old friends, needing only to be transcended; this means that they are not repressed or defeated, but simply subsumed in the Life of Fullness.

As you Practice in this new way, there will be confusion and surprise, as well as the resultant questions, puzzlement, and wonderment. These must be brought to the Guide in the most concrete, innocent form possible; that is, before you have thought much, generalized, or concluded about the particular event. In other words, "Just the facts, ma'am," or just that pure next event in question, how you Practiced, and the confusing or surprising outcome, without any of your judgmental embellishments. In this way, the Guide can help you to go beyond this outcome to the revelation that may be found therein, at least until you are better able to do this yourself.

To begin with, the Practice will seem strange; you will feel awkward behaving in any way that is not normal for you. Acting other than in your familiar, conditioned way will seem awkward, not too different from suddenly finding yourself chosen to act in the school play. Do not be surprised by this, any more than you would in learning a new craft, sport, skill, or art. And, as you know, this awkwardness will diminish as you Practice.

Here, the horse-and-rider analogy will help. Your Lower self-order of functioning is the horse that is wild. You are the rider, who is really your Higher self-order of functioning, which at present you can be aware of only as your Intent in the Practice. There is a destination to reach, and you need the horse to reach it. The wild horse must first be "gentled"; you do not beat it into submission or destroy its spirit. You gradually train it to take the bridle, then lead it around, then mount it, and gradually ride the horse more and more until you eventually get to the point where horse and rider can function as one, under the gentle guidance of the rider. It is much the same with the Practice. At first, your Lower self-order of functioning, which until now you thought of as the whole of you, will rebel at any other authority but its coveted control, so you will have to be patient and gentle, but persistent, in guiding it to accept the Practice as the salvation from its awareness of Despair.

This awareness of the Despair can be a great friend at this point because it continues to serve as a reminder to the Lower self-order of functioning that there is no hope in its old familiar world and that it must go beyond the Life of Survival. It is the Practice, based on your Intent, that makes it possible to embrace the Despair fully and then go beyond. Further, an awareness of your Despair does tend to make you feel miserable, so do not expect that to change overnight. Remember that your feelings are just as conditioned by the enculturation as your mental processes. So, at this point, feeling good or bad is not a useful indicator of how well you are Practicing. Feeling good or bad is a lot like gas in babies: all that is needed is to get it out or express it; neither repressing it nor acting or relying on it is necessary.

The Lower self-order of functioning does not readily give up its cherished, habitual tendency to control all. Experiments in the psychology of learning show that people tend to keep repeating the ways that have in the past been successful even in new situations where these no longer work. My favorite analogy for the Lower self-order of functioning manifesting its control at all costs is that of the character of Sergeant Bilko made famous by Phil Silvers in that old television series. Sergeant Bilko was portrayed as a very clever, worldly wise GI character who was continually scheming in an apparently inspired manner to exercise his considerable talent for control in the absence of the true commander, a colonel portrayed as bumbling and nearly slumbering. This is apt because even if there is a dim awareness of a Higher self-order of functioning, the tendency is to think of it as incompetent because of the conventional view of competence as consisting of control. Each episode of this series was like a morality play as invariably Sergeant Bilko's efforts, even as they appeared successful, would result in hilarious failure.

In similar fashion, your unguided Lower self-order of functioning, while appearing very capable at survival, would haughtily and confidently attempt to control its way to the life beyond survival without success. The point of this analogy is to remind you that the Lower self-order of functioning will not readily surrender its vaunted control. Even while you are Practicing, it will attempt to sneak a little of its old control in, especially when it feels that it has a stake in a particularly desired outcome. This is why eternal vigilance is required; that is, you must be vigilant about Attachment in each next event, relying instead upon the Practice and your Intent.

As I pointed out earlier, you must learn to be amphibious, equally at home functioning in either the Life of Survival or the Life of Fullness. However, the earliest efforts on the Second Journey must focus much more on the work toward the Life of Fullness because the Life of Survival is already very familiar and working well. To begin with, I urge that you locate close enough to the Guide to be able to get together face-to-face whenever needed. It is also a good idea at first to break very temporarily (maybe a week or two) from your everyday routines and relationships in order to learn the framework, foundation, and elements of the Practice, as well as to begin Practicing.

The Second Journey is much like going to a far country or foreign place, and, as tourists are wont to do, you will be tempted to liken or relate everything new to the familiar world of your enculturation or to what is normal. Remember that the Lower self-order of functioning has a large stake in normality, and this tendency must be overcome through the Practice with the aid of the Guide, who can help to reveal the new or unknown realm as you evolve on this journey of discovery.

As with a craft, skill, sport, or art, the Practice cannot readily be learned remotely, and that is why proximity to the Guide is necessary. This learning is done through face-to-face encounters and dialogue with the Guide. Once the Practice is learned well, then proximity may not be as important for learning. This proximity is critical because so much of the learning is based on variables that are not verbal and that are communicated quite mysteriously while you and the Guide are present to one another. This communication is a mystery, but I can point to it. The Guide, in your presence, serves as a temporary channel to the Umbilicum process until you discover, through the Practice, your own channel. Please remember that when I refer to this as a mystery, there is no magic involved; I am simply referring to a transcendent and highly ordered realm, the principles of which you may not yet be aware, although it is of your very nature.

Although the wording of the four questions and answers of the Practice should not be changed without consulting the Guide, it is important to see that these are necessarily approximate articulations that can be changed if the need to do so is determined with the Guide. Nothing is carved in stone. Also, one's grasp of them will, of course, increase and change to understanding in the process of Practicing. Nevertheless, the Lower self-order of functioning requires a quite definite and very definitive Practice to act on in order to learn.

Now, as you proceed on the Second Journey, you will find yourself going through an interesting metamorphosis in regard to how you see, as well as act on, the elements of the Practice. Remember, the answers to the four fundamental questions can be treated as tentative hypotheses, which at first you, like a scientist, will act on in the world *as if* they were true. Then, as you discover how generative of learning they are, you will then act on them *as though* they were true until you subsequently find that they can be acted on without hesitation *as* true. Throughout this transformation, even though the wording may remain unchanged, the four answers will undergo quite dramatic changes in your grasp and subsequent understanding as you discover "the eyes to see and the ears to hear" in this new realm.

An area of considerable confusion that arises in attempting

the Practice is the place of the process we call thinking. Of course, thinking is central to the Life of Survival and to arriving at successful survival. It is also essential to your discovering the limits of that life. Once you begin to Practice, although thinking remains central to your continuing successful survival, it will not be central to the Second Journey. You see, your thinking and culture-bound logic are much like a sausage machine: no matter what the ingredients or input, the output will always be sausages. Thinking is the competent way of manipulating the symbols of a culture-bound mind.

However, on the Second Journey, your mind becomes un-bound and will use different modes to access the Umbilicum and Soul processes. You will recall that the Umbilicum process is not limited by or to the spatiotemporal matrix, and that multiway communicative grid will require your mind to explore some new modalities of knowing. This is what the Guide can help you discover in the Practice, but it is not something that can be articulated satisfactorily here. All that can be done is to point at it briefly.

Oftentimes, when you have been Practicing, the Guide will urge you to *dwell* upon something. The tendency will be to *think* about it, and you will go nowhere or in circles. The distinction between dwelling and thinking has been well emphasized in the Zen, Sufi, and other traditions, literature, and practices. The most helpful way I have found to make this distinction is through the analogy of a house that I want you to investigate and report on back to me. You could do this in either of two ways. You could go to the house as an appraiser would, measuring the square footage of the lot, house, and rooms; count the number of bedrooms, baths, and garages; and report on the type and style of construction, roof, architecture, and such. On the other hand, you could go to the house and dwell in it, being open to and experiencing it and the neighborhood, just being there at differ-ent times and situations. These are two very different ways of exploring the house.

In this analogy, the first way is the equivalent of thinking about something. The second way is the equivalent of dwelling upon it. As you can see, thinking about something immediately imposes existing categories and grids upon it, whereas dwelling allows you to remain open, which becomes your primary stance on the Second Journey, in which Revelation is the central mode of learning. Revelation at this level cannot be received by the old mind that attempts to force it into its set categories and grids; it can come only to the transformed open mind. *To Practice is to be in training for Revelation, and that is how you activate the Soul process in you.*

Let us now review by attempting a brief summary of the Practice and its requisite preconditions. First, there is a bottoming-out experience in regard to the Hope process at the limits of the third level of awareness. This comes after you have achieved successful survival, which can give you the strength and confidence so necessary to go beyond the Life of Survival. That can result in an awareness of your Despair and lead to a willingness to turn toward the unknown and to embrace Despair through the clear focus of your Intent. Thus begins the Second Journey, which requires that you first traverse No-man's-land, which entails turning *from* what you consider to be the comfortable known and *to* the unknown of your *Areté.* In order to open yourself up to the Life of Fullness and to inhibit the Life of Survival conditionings that can work as impediments to this journey, you will require the Practice.

The Practice is articulated best by the answers to four fundamental questions: *Who am I? Why am I here? Where am I?* and *What am I to do?* The answers that have been set down here are the simplest, optimal articulations in our limited language framework, and may be regarded as tentative hypotheses to be acted on.

Prior to these four questions and answers is the foundation: your Intent, which must be to "Yearn *first* for the Kingdom of Heaven." Your Intent and the Practice are essential for embarking on the Second Journey. Learning and memorizing the elements and framework of the Practice are necessary but not sufficient to begin this journey; it must then be acted on until the Practice becomes the new conditioning, able to inhibit the old conditioning when it is not needed for survival. You are thus not only able to traverse No-man's-land successfully but are then also open to the revelations to be found through the processes and outcomes of the Practice.

These processes and outcomes will be confusing, puzzling, or a source of wonderment to your enculturated mind, and you will need to bring these to the Guide, who can help you transcend the old conditionings and go on to the Life of Fullness. Thus, you and the Guide must be in proximity, at least during the earlier stages, until proficiency at Practicing has been achieved. As you proceed, your grasp and subsequent understanding of the Practice will change dramatically as the Life of Fullness is realized and lived.

12

EPILOGUE: BEYOND
THE PRACTICE —
METANOIA

*I*n the first half of this book, I emphasized the importance
of becoming aware of an *ecology of the mind, heart, and body*.
Such an ecology, in keeping with the Greek root of the term, is
concerned with our inner household or environment, as well as
with our continuing reactions thereto. This requires an awareness of both the resources available and the extensive pollution
that has been produced within. As with external ecology, we tend
to become aware of the pollution first, which has the effect of
alarming us. This leads us first to consider what our lives would
be like without such pollutants and then to become aware of and
use our available resources wisely. It was in this manner that I
have proceeded.

We have discovered the terrible burden of pollution the heart,
mind, and body carry as a result of our enculturation, especially
the burden imposed by the Fear and Hope processes, together
with their associated conditionings, that serve to limit us to the
Life of Survival and its derivative values of the First Journey.

Discovering these pollutants, their sources, and how they preclude the full enjoyment of our inner resources was vital to this inquiry. Up to that point, the focus was on a new understanding of what I have called human norms and their consequences for us.

Like its offspring, industrialization, which has contributed mightily to our continued, assured survival, our enculturation has been necessary to learning successful survival. However, even at the heights of their successes, both have also yielded withering, polluting ecological disasters. Such an awareness of inner disaster can lead us to examine our inward life, but this cannot be done by using the usual failed approaches: we require a more open, generative way to discover that which will be new to us.

So, we then went on to explore the resources available, which I have called human nature—more emphatically, *emergent human nature*—which cannot be discovered using the framework and methodology that were successful with human norms. An entirely new, more appropriate framework and methodology is required, and that has been the focus of the second half of this book. Our framework involved the Yearning, the Questing, the Umbilicum process, the Lower self-order of functioning, and the Higher self-order of functioning, as well as the four levels of awareness. Our methodology consisted of the Practice based upon the foundation of our Intent. This simply entails our choosing to act on the latest mutation of our emergent human nature, the Soul process, which we are here to realize on our Second Journey to the Life of Fullness. This inward way involves a path that is unique to each one taking that journey; these inner resources need to be discovered, at first with the aid of the Guide, through the Practice.

The point of Practicing is *Redemption*, as well as *Salvation*, two very old words that are reclaimed from their languishing in either the hell of misuse or the purgatory of disuse. You need to redeem something when it is in hock or in captivity, and that is the condition of the world of your consciousness. Before the Second Journey, this is the whole world for each of us and the only world you can do anything about. But why does it need redeeming? Very simply, because it is in hock to or the captive of an illusory view—namely, your version of the worldview of your enculturation. In that illusory view, you are convinced that the Life of Survival is the totality and that you must control your way to success therein as the sole or major purpose of your life. This meager view of life must be transcended by redeeming your consciousness from this captivity. The coin of this Redemption is your Intent, acted on in the Practice. Remarkably, when this process of Redemption is done through the Practice and you transcend to the Life of Fullness, it will feel as if you have been freed from captivity. It is exhilarating!

Salvation is another appropriate term to describe what is needed when your Soul process is detained or kept from proceeding by its captivity. So, you need to be saved from the control of the limited Lower self-order of functioning that either denies or distorts the Yearning for your *Areté*, which is the Soul process. Otherwise, you are led inexorably to a stunted life dominated by distractions and diversions, and then to ennui in later life.

Whether I speak of Redemption or Salvation, I am talking about the world of your consciousness, which requires a radical change in awareness in order to realize the Life of Fullness that is your birthright, if you will just claim it. This has also been called higher consciousness or transconsciousness, or *Metanoia* by the ancient Greeks. Such dramatic changes in awareness have been described in the literature as the process of enlightenment or rebirth. It can be considered rebirth because your first birth is an ordinary one into the Life of Survival, but this is an extraordinary new birth into the Life of Fullness. Or, it can be considered enlightenment because even at the limits of the third level of awareness, the most you have are glimpses or whispers—or "seeing through a glass darkly"—whereas this is like seeing the Truth face-to-face at noon on a clear day. This is the process of discovering who you really are in relationship to the Cosmos and to the Source ultimately. What else is this but enlightening?

With the awareness arrived at through the Practice, you let the Higher self-order of functioning come into its rightful dominion in your life. The meagerness of your former life of control pales in contrast to such a dominion. Your Higher self-order of functioning is guided by and expresses a simple yet ineffable principle, which can be pointed at by the term *Divine Love*. It is Divine Love that you are in training for in the Practice, and it is best articulated as "responding according to the needs of the situation." As we have discussed, this points at the highest Love imaginable. Once you get past the childishness of the ascendancy of wants and conditioned desires, you can arrive at the mature wisdom of Love, which you can discover and come to express, both within and without, through the Practice.

There are myriad ways of pointing at this principle of Divine Love. One that I can articulate here is the subprinciple, or corollary, that *every one of our needs is met*. This is a principle that can be grasped, not without difficulty at first, and which can be understood only by discovering it yourself through the Practice. That "every one of our needs is met" seems an outlandish statement in view of your past experiences. Of course, it does not appear true when your awareness is under the control of the Lower self-order of functioning, where you filter all of your perceptions through the agenda of your very limited Life of Survival goals and purposes. Thus, all too often, you reject that which comes to meet your need.

Consider, for example, the situation where nearly everything seems to be going wrong in your life. Then, as though to add insult to injury, a valued relationship or situation begins to go awry. Instead of simply yielding *aikido*-like (*aikido* has been aptly called the loving art of self-defense), you resist and fight it tooth and nail, when very likely that situation or relationship needs to change so that something or someone you truly need can enter your life. Acting on your reactions in this manner obscures the awareness of your needs being met. Seeing the truth that each of your needs is met is precluded by your captive awareness, until you have attained the grander, transcendent view of the Higher self-order of functioning in dominion as the result of redeeming your world or consciousness through the Practice.

The Higher self-order of functioning has to be chosen by *letting* it come into dominion in your life. When that occurs, then your *Areté* unfolds unfettered by the inhibitions and shackles of your previously exclusive reliance on the Lower self-order of functioning. Remember, all of your conditioning that is needed for the Life of Survival remains intact and continues to be available to you, but the now well-trained Lower self-order of functioning does not attempt its control beyond the realm of survival. The horse-and-rider analogy is apt here again. The horse is your Lower self-order of functioning, and you ride it at your will and not the other way around, which would be grotesque at the least. The horse and rider must be in proper relationship for this journey.

In fact, all of your conditioning, including the Fear and Hope processes, will remain with you. The difference is that you will know, through the Practice, what to do with them and when to use them. You will use whatever conditioning is needed for continued successful survival as long as it does not conflict with your Intent. Any other conditionings that come up will be treated as the reactions they are and will not be acted upon as you Practice. Recall that the point of the Practice is not just to become a perfect practitioner, but to take you beyond it to the Life of Fullness.

As I have said, when the Higher self-order of functioning comes into dominion, it can only be by your choice or letting. It does not force itself upon you, but is simply your birthright which you need to claim. The concept of the Grace of God is appropriate here, so let us rescue it for our use. The Grace of God is said to flow freely and at all times; in other words, God is always calling to us. This is just another, older way of saying that we are sons/daughters of God who Loves us, who is always responding according to the needs of our situation, and that this Love is always available to us. What more apt personification of this process—the Source—could there be than that of a Loving Father—or better, that of a Loving Parent or Mother-Father, since gender here is no part of the reality. When you become aware of and accept this Love or the Grace of God, then God or the Source is in you and comes to your awareness when you choose or claim your birthright. God can come only in dominion, and this is who you really are: the Higher self-order of functioning in dominion over your Lower self-order of functioning.

At this point begins the truly grand adventure that cannot be articulated, but I can point at it with an analogy. Life becomes much like an ongoing play, continuously being written, directed, staged, and produced by your very best, most-trusted friend, as you star or Play in it. You have no idea what will happen, but it is always wondrous, and you will marvel at the amazing juxtapositions of people and events. Actually, this is what has been going on all along, but until you start Practicing, all you can do with the Lower self-order of functioning in control is to interfere with the unfolding of this play. By Practicing, you quit interfering and begin to learn the principles that operate or guide in this new realm. For science-fiction buffs, beginning to Practice is like going to a new planet in another galaxy or dimension, where events do not follow the principles of your accustomed world, but where, once you get past trying to fit everything into your old worldview, you have the opportunity to discover the new principles that operate there.

The answers to the four fundamental questions in the Practice are simply attempts in our limited language system to articulate these new principles of the Life of Fullness. Recall that I likened these four answers to the four corners of a structure to be built upon the foundation of your Intent. As you Practice, this structure is taking form; in other words, you are discovering principles that are new to you. But something very interesting occurs in this building process. As you become proficient in the Practice and attain to letting the Higher self-order of functioning come into dominion, you will realize that this is no ordinary structure. The four answers or principles of the Practice have become one, and your structure has assumed the shape of a pyramid (an ancient way of alluding to this mystery), the four corners having risen to a single point. This single point is the Principle underlying and overlaying the Cosmos, variously pointed to by such terms as *God*, the *Ultimate*, *Nirvana*, the *Tao*, *Love*, and many others. That single Principle is truly a mystery, which can be pointed at by the term *Love*, but which can be known only by your discovering and exploring it in the Life of Fullness.

That is the mystery the mystic sets out to explore. The mystic is the practical one who has discovered the limits of the Life of Survival and who has embarked on the Second Journey. This journey, as I have tried to show here, is how you can become aware of an inner ecology of the body, mind, and heart so necessary to beginning the Soul process. What could be more practical than this? The mystic will not settle for the illusoriness and the deception of an unredeemed life.

The mystic is also often misunderstood as one who withdraws from life. This is no more a withdrawal than going on to college or graduate school is a withdrawal from the previous level. On the contrary, embarking on the Second Journey requires great courage to attempt to go beyond the familiar and conventionally comfortable. This is the *Courage to Be*, to borrow Paul Tillich's phrase and book title. It is the courage to be who you really are in your Higher self-order of functioning—not the ersatz identities of your Lower self-order of functioning.

Discovering who you really are through the Practice results in the deepest understanding of the mystery of the *Golden Rule* of doing unto others as you would have them do unto you. Acting on the answers to the four fundamental questions leads to loving one another—not with that weak sentimentality we normally call love, but with that powerful and empowering Divine Love that is truly the Power and the Glory for which you are here.

Divine Love enables us to recognize one another as members of that one family of humankind that is One with the Source through the Umbilicum process. Without such awareness, we have to settle in this world for human justice, which is so crude and can often be cruel, mechanistic, ineffective, and regressive. With such awareness, however, we can discover Divine Justice, in which we treat one another as we would ourselves, recognizing who we really are. Human justice, no matter how evolved, results in the society and world that we currently endure and deplore. This is the Hell of our inner ecological pollution, which we experience both within (psychologically and spiritually) and without (sociopolitically). We have been created for the Heaven of the Life of Fullness of which we are heirs and need only to claim it. Our time here may seem surprisingly short, but the Life of Fullness is far beyond a fair tradeoff for life's brevity. The Life of Fullness is your *Areté* to which you are being pulled or drawn by the Yearning, if you will but admit it to your awareness.

Instead, clamoring for your attention from all sides are reports of the many-faceted tragedy that is afflicting humanity. To compound this human tragedy, professionals, politicians, academics, mass media, and a plethora of books being issued alarm us daily to take the old, tried and true problem-solving approach, which works fine for technology and the Life of Survival. But we must go beyond problem-solving to discover that "life is not a problem to be solved but a mystery to be lived," an underlying theme of this entire work.

"He was sent to redeem the world" is an expression of the mystery to be lived, and it is true of each one of us who becomes aware of the Yearning.

If you do choose—
and the choice is entirely yours—
you are here to redeem the world of your consciousness
which has been in thrall to such a meager unreality
that is so unworthy of your true emergent human nature———
your SOUL.

Index

About the Author

George Jaidar is known for his startling and original work in emergent human nature and consciousness in the Post-religious Era. This book, and Jaidar's Courage To Be workshops, explore the cultural and psychological bases of humanity's evolution to a new level of spiritual unfoldment, for which religion was an early, "kindergarten" stage.

Born in Amyoun-el-koura, Lebanon, Jaidar grew up in Uruguay and California. Starting as an altar boy in the Eastern Orthodox Church, but deeply in uenced by his grandmother's stories in the Su tradition, he embarked on a life-long spiritual quest that involved extensive study of Eastern and Western philosophy, psychology, and religion, with particular emphasis on the mystic way that transcends all religious traditions.

Jaidar received his BA in Psychology from Stanford University, was an instructor trainer in the U.S. Air Force during the Korean War, and later became a real estate broker, builder and developer. However, his success in business and community service (including leading Liberal Arts discussion groups for UCLA, Kiwanis Club, and political and professional organizations,) and even marriage and two children did not meet his deep inner yearning. Jaidar decided to return to teaching, working four years toward a Ph.D. in Philosophy at UCLA, while also on the staff of the Department of Liberal Arts.

Subsequently a headmaster of a college-prep school, and then an educational consultant, Jaidar has worked for the past 25 years primarily with individuals and small groups, encouraging growth toward what Jaidar calls the Life of the Spirit or the "Life of Fullness." Drawing from his rich background in teaching philosophy, psychology, cultural anthropology, and comparative religions, as well as his grounding in both Eastern and Western mystical traditions, *Jaidar proclaims the Soul-process as an emergent mutation of human consciousness: the next stage of our spiritual evolution.*

Just as Mind evolved out of and subsumed Body, Soul is evolving out of and subsumes Mind. Unlike the conventional view of evolution, Jaidar shows how this nascent stage must be chosen and embarked upon by each individual. It is necessary to go beyond the comfortable known of an enculturated worldview which can go no further than ensuring survival, if that. Such a transformative journey requires courage, and George Jaidar's book and workshops explore the requisites and the rst steps on this adventure in emergent human nature and consciousness.